ꝗ Cheated Death

real life miracles through the goodness of God

cover photography by Beth M. Rogers

I Cheated Death

real life miracles through the goodness of God

Greta Kataha-Spica

PUBLISHING CO.

Rutledge, Alabama

I Cheated Death

ISBN 978-1514726853

First Edition
Published July 2015
Around the Loop Publishers
1668 W Third Street
Luverne, AL 36049
www.aroundtheloopdesigns.com

Dedication

This book of my many breathtaking testimonies "I Cheated Death" is dedicated to my Lord and Saviour Jesus Christ, the Author and Finisher of my faith. He was my anchor and the Main Hero all through the pages. I believe countless souls will be added into the Kingdom of God for His glory!

All poetry and songs are Holy Spirit inspired and composed by Greta, unless otherwise noted.

Acknowledgments

My Children: Belinda, Roy, Jesse and Rachel Ruth inspired me to write this book that will bless them, my grandchildren and great-grandkids for generations to come. They are my unique gifts, precious jewels and miracle blessings from the Lord who helped me persevere and walk closer to my Lord Jesus Christ every day. I believe these real life miracles, an interesting book of records will be a valuable asset, settle doubts, answer questions and bring back memories of joy. It is a reminder of the goodness, faithfulness and amazing love of Yahweh God that surpasses all understanding. Thank you Darling Darlings, you make me so proud and a blessed Mama always!

I appreciate and thank my husband and bestest friend, Fred Spica for taking up the challenge to run this race with me. A man after God's own heart, he encouraged and prayed with me through out this project. With great joy together we shall continue to serve our Lord and King!

I bring to remembrance a man who was my Mentor, Coach, Pastor, Husband, Friend and the Father to all my Children, Late Apollo Kataha who never gave up on me. Our endless love together with the Holy Spirit has made all this possible for God was always with us!

Introduction

It is my privilege and honor to write this book. I like to share with you all of my real life stories. You will know my days of struggles, hardships and triumphs. Victory was written all over my life even before I took my first breath on this earth. I had far too many difficulties but I dared to live and cheated death many times over. I suffered greatly from birth to adulthood, as a young woman, a widow and as a minister of the Gospel of Jesus Christ. Experiences from my inter-racial marriage, stories of war, death, grief and loss may have left many scars in my life but I never gave up. I could not afford to give up. I had no choice but to hold on to hope. I faced every hardship, fear and hurdle as they came along. Times I wanted to disappear, to sleep and never wake up. But somehow, something kept me holding on. However difficult my situations were, I never let my situations hold me down.

When anguish and despair knocked me off my feet, I tried hard to pick myself up again. I tried to destroy myself, run away and pretend but there it was; danger, fear, depression and desperation tried to paralyze me but the supernatural hand of God rescued me. Angels and strangers came my way in most amazing ways from nowhere. Discouragement gave me an opportunity to understand God's grace. My weaknesses gave me courage to rely on God. I learned to fight for life and for love from a very early age and all through my marriage. I was cornered from all sides, words may fail to describe certain situations but for God I would have failed. I took bold risks and with determination I held on to my dreams. I did the best I knew how and prayed to keep my marriage together and to see my family alive again. My whole life was a challenge from one stage to another, but finally I started seeing victory after victory after victory. Life may not seem easy but with God all things are possible.

I have tried time and time again to tell my story in bits and pieces, but never dreamed I would be writing this book. Too many obstacles came my way from the very start to finish. Even though I was healed over and over again, the memories were fresh. The wounds would begin to bleed and I take a deep breath of relief and know it was all over. The worst was gone and now I can continue to face tomorrow with joy. Weeping may come in the night but Joy comes in the morning. It's good to share testimonies; contemplating, remembering that the miracle stories of God bring sweet healing and restoration. It gives comfort and joy in this journey of life. You will see that you are not the only one suffering in this world we temporarily call home. It is a part of living, striving to hold on to family and working towards a good marriage. People have different circumstances than others. It depends how you handle each situation. When we speak about our hurts, fears and disappointments, healing will be complete. We must expose darkness and share our stories so others can understand life. Healing will take place from the inside out. The reason you have come across this book is not an accident. It will help you help others in their healing process. The Holy Spirit will touch your mind, emotions and free your soul. Like an onion, the layers will come off one by one, the wounds will heal and you can boast of your triumphs in Christ. What He has done for you. Build your confidence in Jesus who alone can changed your direction and rewrite your life's story. How ready are you to make change? YOU can rewrite the destiny of your marriage, your children, your family and your nation. God is changing your story dramatically to impact the lives of so many more searching for answers.

Be encouraged, in life's struggles you are not alone! No situation is too difficult for you to handle. Regardless of all you go through, you can move on. You can make it. Every cloud has a silver lining. No matter how dark the tunnel may be, there is light at the end of it. Light will show up, it has to show up. It's not over till God says it's over. Whatever you face, you can bounce right back. I'm a witness. I've been there and done that. Beaten down too many times but I was determined to get up, dust off and keep moving. Every test and trial will come to an end. The wounds will eventually heal and you will be stronger than before. Your scars will soon be reminders for celebration. Your mess will become a message to release other people from their messy situations. Tests will be testimonies to inspire others. Every setback can be turned into success and each stumbling block into stepping stones. Setbacks cannot stop your success. In the sentence of life, a setback is a COMMA - not a PERIOD. Setbacks are temporary. Setback is a setup for a comeback; stronger, brighter and sweeter. You need to step out of your comfort zone and take risks. No situation is permanent. Don't give up! Change will come. They simply cannot stay. You must endure for a while so life can get better with time. You will shine in your darkest hour and grow in wisdom, knowledge and understanding. God is able to bring out the best in you. You will overcome and be victorious.

These are days of great distress, violence, sexual abuse, perversion and injustice especially towards women and children. But this is not new. It has been an age old violation, unspeakable truth and many young girls and older women try to brush it aside out of fear or too much pain. Through the years many carry a heavy load of guilt, insecurity, unsatisfactory marriages and incomplete homes. Many precious lives suffer these scars and some take them to the grave. But there is help and there is hope. Jesus Christ suffered like a man in all things and He can carry you through when you put your faith in Him. If you have not suffered pain, shame, rejection or fear, know that at some point in life it will find you. You may be facing a peculiar situation, family struggle, marriage or the death of a loved one. But no matter how hard, helpless and dreadful your circumstances maybe, you will come out of it.

This world is quickly turning into a small global village. We are able to connect with people from different walks of life, all across the world right from where we are. People are interacting, intermarrying and exchanging cultures every hour. There is an urgency to prepare generations to come with our life experiences so they are not thrown off balance. When the going gets tough, the tough will keep going. The Bible says, "That which has been is what will be, that which is done is what will be done, and there is nothing new under the sun." Ecclesiastes 1:9. For this very reason, I like you to journey with me and see how God showed up and showed off at every crossroad in my life. As you walk with me with an open mind, you will be encouraged to think and act differently; towards inter-racial marriages, mixed cultures, colored families, women, children, religion and various ethnic groups. You will witness the struggles and victories of family living even in the midst of dire hardships. You may be able to glean valuable nuggets and secret truths from my life threatening experiences.

Once you are determined to move on, no excuse can hold you back. Your life will turn around for good. Every experience will become a lesson for success. Your later days will be better than the former. No one can erase your past. You may never forget the yesteryears but you can rewrite your future. Fight for what is rightfully yours like a wild lioness fighting for her cubs. Face life one day at a time, step by step and you will begin to see things differently. Trials and tests are inevitable, but what you do with them makes the difference. Instead of getting bitter, let them help you get better. Let them soften your heart to love even more. They will equip you for promotion and prepare you for the next level of your blessings. God's plan will unfold which is far greater than this world can ever dream of. Every scar is a badge of honor for all eternity. Jesus exchanged everything in our lives. He gave us faith over fear, healing over grief and pain, prosperity over poverty, love over strive, peace over confusion, joy over sorrow, abundance over losses and blessings over curses. The Holy Spirit of might and power moved every mountain in my life to make His joy complete and real. What He has done for us, He will do for you! Get ready, get set and let's go!

You have allowed me to suffer much hardship,
but you will restore me to life again and
lift me up from the depths of the earth.
You will restore me to even greater honor
and comfort me once again.

Psalm 71:20-21.

Letter of Appreciation

It is with great pleasure that I take this opportunity to convey my deepest appreciation to my beloved Sister Greta Kahata-Spica, a true faithful servant of the Lord Jesus Christ. I first met her and her faithful loving husband, the late Brother Apollo (May he rest in peace. Amen) in 1990 when they became members of the Full Gospel Church of Philadelphia in the Manama Bahrain in the Middle East. They both had an undeniable calling of the Lord upon their lives which caused me to ordain Brother Apollo to preach and teach the Word of God. They both were leaders and Ministers of the Bahrain Awali, Friday Night Fellowship. Sister Greta also ministered and served the women in the Nurse's Hostels. As their ministry expanded and time went on they decided to migrate to Ontario Canada and before their departure the Executive Church Council Elders, Deacons and I held an official ordination ceremony to bestow God's blessings upon them.

In 2007 we received the sad news about our beloved Brother Apollo and Minister of the Gospel saying good bye to the world and claiming his mansion in heaven. Sister Greta and her children continued on with the ministry the Lord had assigned them. Later on, the Lord blessed Sister Greta with a godly husband, Evangelist Fred Spica, and raised the Hearts Ablaze Ministry for the glory of God. It's a blessing to hear that she has authored a book titled "I Cheated Death" that most certainly will bless the Body of Christ. As a Pastor I have supported her mission work in India and other places and continue to pray for the entire family as the Lord continues to expand their ministry.

In His Love, Mercy and Compassion.

Evangelista Victor Rosado, South Carolina, USA
(*Former Senior Pastor, of Full Gospel Church of Philadelphia, Bahrain*)

To my Mama, You are the pillar of this family and your leadership as a wife, mother, grandmother and a servant of God will be spoken of ever after you are gone. Thank you for always being you and never wavering from the truth and passion God has placed within your heart. You are mighty fearless but yet compassionate and gracious Lioness that God has ordained anointed and set a part for such a time as this. Enjoy these days mama. No more sorrow no more grief, no more pain. You Graduated and overcame one of the toughest seasons of your life and remember it's the crown of life that awaits you in this age and in the age to come.

Love you ma!

Your son,

Jesse Kataha

Contents

Chapter 1 19

Chapter 2 33

Chapter 3 53

Chapter 4 67

Chapter 5 89

Chapter 6 107

Chapter 7 137

Chapter 8 161

Testimonies and Praise Reports 177

Hearts Ablaze Worldwide Ministries 208

Chapter One

I awoke to the sound of pouring rain running down my window pane. The rain was beating hard as if to break my window. I jumped up and realized it was only a dream! There was no rain but we had a beautiful sunny day. Most Holy Spirit dreams are for a specific purpose. This dream was not like many others I could barely remember. But there was a significant message here that reminded me it was time to share a "fire encounter" I had with the Holy Spirit in spring of 1999. Rain signifies the outpouring of the Holy Spirit as promised in Joel 2:28-32. I will pour out my Spirit on all flesh. Rain also represents cleansing and purification. After heavy "rains" there's usually a great harvest. The two outpourings of the Spirit are referred to as the first (or former) rain and the last (or latter) rain. The Spirit was poured out in the former rain at Pentecost. The latter rain will bring an abundant harvest of souls and a cleansing in the Church. For the earth which drinks in the rain that often comes upon it, and bears herbs useful for those by whom it is cultivated, receives blessing from God. In my vision I saw an end time Baptism of Fire spread and consume the nations, people and individuals like never before. Since then the fire of Christ's amazing love has compelled me to challenge God's people to be "hot on fire" for the Lord. Revelation 3:16. Fire is also a refiner that is sent to separate and sanctify the Church as we wait for the return of Jesus.

Suffering Through The Anointing

My flesh was in agony from a rotting skin disease. The skin on both my legs, from knee down suddenly began to itch, crack and bleed. I used every type of lotion and treatment available, consulted dermatologists and specialists about my condition but they could not diagnose anything except to give me an ointment for the irritation. It was not an allergic reaction because only my lower legs were raw. I tried everything to ease the pain and went from one specialist to another. I wore long skirts or pants during the day and wrapped my legs in plastic at night because of the rotten stench and irritation. This went on for almost a year. Day and night my husband Apollo would weep and pray over my legs and we began to seek God for answers. "It is hard to accept the fact that there is nothing we can do with suffering except to suffer it." Such was my condition. Prayer was our only answer. I was an active working wife, mother of four and a co-labourer with my husband in the Kingdom of God.

At the same time something strange was happening within my spirit. I had a desperate longing to spend time alone with God. In the beginning I was afraid and could not understand the Holy Spirit's intercession that would overtake me even in my sleep. Like a pregnant woman in labour my stomach would tighten as if to push in prayer and all I could do is open my mouth, whimper, groan and weep. Months later, I started working for the Benny Hinn Ministries, in Toronto and prayed with the staff regularly. Every day, all I wanted to do was hurry home, lock myself away and wait. A heavy, tangible presence and a burning would penetrate my being. "This was a little similar to my first experience in our home in the Middle East. My salvation was not in a prayer I said but I was filled with the Holy Spirit and started speaking in a strange tongue when I secretly desired for the truth." Now, as I begin to quietly pray in the spirit my sighs would turn into groans and uncontrollable weeping. Although there was discomfort and pain in my body because of soreness, it didn't bother me when I was in prayer. At first, we did not understand the connection between this rotting skin condition and my spiritual experience. But several months later when I stepped out in faith and obeyed my calling to start a "Woman Ablaze Ministry" in Canada, God supernaturally healed my skin. Gradually the itching and bleeding stopped, the wounds closed up and I was able to walk again without pain. The scars tell my God stories. This has nothing to do with the vessel but it is our heavenly Father's heart for His children. It is the emotional expression of the Holy Spirit to save people in these last days. Many do not understand such moving of the Spirit. So not to allow others to sin against the Holy Spirit and to mock, laugh or reject Him in us, we held on to these experiences, visions and dreams until it was time to share them openly. Some Pastors, Leaders and Saints in the Western world are still not able to comprehend the manifestations and the supernatural working of the Holy Spirit. But the Bible clearly explains this in Romans 8:26 The groanings of the Holy Spirit are best described as warfare prayers and pleas made according to the will of the Father.

Intimacy with Jesus has drawn me into another level in my walk with the Lord. I hear God through dreams and open visions and receive specific words of wisdom, knowledge, instructions and understanding for Kingdom purposes. In many of my dreams I am carried in the spirit to deliver and pray for the oppressed in other parts of the world. I visit hospitals, churches and the streets to rescue women and hear children, girls and babies crying out for help in my spirit. When in prayer or fellowship, certain parts of my body will burn as an indication to listen to God or to discern and pray for the anguish and needs in people's lives. We started the first Women's breakfast in May of 2000 in the church we attended and later moved it to our house. Every third Saturday of the month women of all faiths came to our home for fellowship and open house breakfast. The Lord provided more than we needed. This opened new doors for ministry and other outreach programs. We distributed food, warm clothing and household items to new immigrants, single families and seniors in our Community.

Every time a situation arises, the Lord takes me into a place of groaning intercession. I am blessed to be used in such a unique way, an honour I do not take lightly. This calling is the most awesome gift one can ever receive, it is holy and sacred no words can describe. Jesus wept bitterly over Jerusalem, in the garden before His crucifixion and even now He intercedes on our behalf. God is looking for prayer warriors who are willing to stand in the gap for someone else's need, to pray for an adverse situation that may be developing or for lost souls. It was obvious that God was doing a good work in our family and ministry. The home Bible study and prayer group was growing. People from all faiths were being delivered from demonic oppression, witchcraft and bondage. The Lord led us deeper into deliverance and healing to restore lives. Believers Deliverance Church and Ministry was birthed in the basement of our home in Canada on November 4th, 2000. We started with seven people, grew out of the rented public facility and relocated to the South Common Community Center in Mississauga Ontario.

I Cheated Death

Tsunami Wildfire Revolution

During one of these intimate times with Jesus, I was caught up in a vision of a wildfire spreading fast over the people all across the earth. A mighty wind rapidly carried this overwhelming tsunami-like wildfire all across the nations and people were consumed in it. Some were baptized in this fire in awe and excitement while others fled in fear and were destroyed. Women were rising from a fetal position (backs curved, head bowed, and the limbs bent and drawn up to the torso) and standing upright with new boldness. Youth were loosed from chains of bondage and ran with a banner of Jesus across the streets. A fear came over the land yet no one was able to control or dare stop this fire. Before ascending to the Father, Jesus promised His disciples the gift of the Holy Spirit and power, Acts 1:8. God is preparing a spiritual tsunami to sweep the nations and reclaim our culture for Christ. Each one of us has a special assignment in this mission in taking back the nations for the Kingdom of God. We are in the final stages of labour and birth pangs are getting stronger now than ever before. He who is able to hear, let him listen to and heed what the Spirit says to the assemblies (churches). He who overcomes (is victorious) shall in no way be injured by the second death. Revelation 2:11. A shaking is already happening and a Tsunami Wildfire Revolution is about to consume the earth just I was shown in my vision fifteen years ago.

Groaning, Travailing Intercession

All Christians are called to prayer and intercession, but an ordained intercessor is able to bear the burden of Christ in a way that no other can. Not many understand this calling. A burden and pain is generated from deep within the intercessor's innermost being, which is called in scriptures "bowels of Jesus Christ," Philippians 1:8. They enter into a realm where the desires and burdens of Christ become alive in their spirit, soul and body. That means they literally feel the pain of the agony of the Holy Spirit. This is why the prayer of an intercessor is called "travailing prayer" or "agonizing prayer". The Bible says the Holy Spirit literally helps us to pray and pleads in our behalf with unspeakable yearnings and groanings too deep to be uttered in words. Romans 8:26. Casual prayers are done with eloquent words, while intercessory prayer is done with weeping, mourning, agonizing and travail; as in labour just before childbirth. For this, we must have a personal bond, an intimacy with Jesus

22

to possess His heart of compassion for others. Then what breaks the heart of God will break ours too.

Divine Map For My Journey

Born in South India, I have traveled extensively and lived most of my life in East Africa, the Middle East and in North America. Its mind boggling to think how God brought me from the third world to a first world nation. Rags to riches, poverty to abundance and from darkness to His marvelous light, He carried me through for such a time as this. We all have a rag story, a tale to tell, something unpleasant, hurting and bad. But only Jesus can turn the woes into worship and sadness into joy. Such miracle stories hold me in awe of the faithfulness and goodness of God. Only a loving, heavenly Father can bring our desires, dreams and hopes into reality, more than we can ask, think or imagine. Ephesians 3:20. God's divine map for my journey changed my entire destiny and life itself. These stories are not to accuse or discredit anyone but they lift up the name of Jesus. I have learned to forgive myself, forgive others and to receive His forgiveness every day. Dead or alive we must forgive our loved ones and those who have done us wrong. When we do not or cannot forgive, we drag that person around and carry our garbage bag everywhere we go. Until we forgive and break off soul ties of the past, we cannot move on to better things that are waiting for us.

Marriage Works

Many of these supernatural wonders are nothing short but miraculous! Good, bad, sad and the ugly. You think the bad and sad will never end but they do. My stories may not be of sexual abuse, continuous rape, sex trafficking, drugs, murder or divorce like that is so common today. But I am a witness to even such hateful things in the lives of others. My testimonies are real life experiences that women and families face from day to day. "Marriage and love has no excitement, nothing to gain if everything was good and perfect. If there is no fight to keep the 'Love Story' going, forever sealed till death parts Husband and Wife." Perhaps perfection is not in this world but with Jesus the perfect, eternal Bridegroom, the Lover of all lovers! Marriage takes hard work to keep up the vows we made on our wedding day. To have and to hold, from this day forward, for better, for worse, for richer, for poorer, in sickness or in health, to love and to cherish 'till death do us part'. We strived not only in the good times but also in the bad times; in hopelessness, helplessness and homelessness. Sacrifice, endurance, perseverance and persistence works even in an interracial family. It may not be easy but when we try our best God does the rest.

Everyone else gave up on us and told us to quit but we hoped and trusted in God. I followed my husband through thick and thin. Like Ruth followed Naomi and pleaded; for wherever you go, I will go; and wherever you lodge, I will lodge; your people shall be my people, and your God, my God If anything but death parts you and me. Ruth 1:16-17. Separation and struggles are hard but love can help us conquer anything. Many like to be that Proverbs 31 woman, wife and mother and quote the scriptures but few understand the price, the battles and struggles it takes to hold a family together. This scripture talks about trust, reliance, discernment, wisdom, hard work, praise from her children and respect and honour for her husband. But such a woman must walk continually in worship and fear of a holy God. A woman who fears the Lord shall be praised! This is the key to any relationship. The reverential fear of the Lord is sweet and brings a good aroma to God's nostrils. As we draw closer to God we draw closer to our spouse and together we make Jesus the center of everything and He makes Marriage work. Beautifully said but this takes working in faith, forgiveness and unconditional love.

Stories Unfold

From an unwanted baby to a rejected teenage girl, I learned early to play dangerously with life. A broken home, an alcoholic father and a stench of immorality can cause a young person to go downhill. I was searching for love in all the wrong places, hurting men along the way. Because I was hurt I couldn't trust any man. As the saying goes; "hurting people hurt other people." Risk was the name of my game that led me from one battle ground to another. On several occasions I attempted to take my own life but even death ran away from me. My circumstances and family said I would never make it. In my twenties and I was already fed up of life. I simply had to go away from all the hurt, shame and blame. Escape myself far from family and from everything around me. I was recovering from a nasty accident, a broken engagement and the loss of my father. This was my breaking point. Something had to happen and quickly.

24

Some stories are easy to tell while others are sensitive, too deep and sore to the mind. No young girl or woman should suffer what I've been through. No one told me that grief felt like fear, like an amputation and the pain never goes away. Poverty is a curse passed from generation to generation and it cannot be a blessing as we were made to believe. Even so, God can heal any fear, pain and lack. The blessings of the Lord make one rich and He adds no sorrow to them. Riches are not only in money and wealth but in everything that makes our joy complete. You will look towards heaven and see that every blessing comes from God. Stop striving and start praising the One from whom all blessings flow. You will enjoy what I share and learn about other cultures, hate discrimination, embrace mixed marriages, love people of all faiths and understand what compels others to do what they do. In all things love wins. Everyone has the same emotions, needs and capacity for love and to be loved. We cannot, must not be afraid to help others. To save those who are beaten down by society, family and Church; to help rescue women off the streets, let men know their priestly position in a home and to teach our youth, boys and girls how valuable they are. Each person is uniquely different. This life can get pretty tough, unfair and cruel in this world we temporarily call home. But for God my life would be in ruins and my soul on its way to hell. Mercy and grace kissed in my favour.

God's Voice Is Real

Urgency in the voice of God quickens me to pack these breathtaking testimonies in a book and publish them to the world. For some time, I've been procrastinating in discouragement, giving one excuse after another. But now there is need to share my life stories so more people can live and love freely. We are a blessed generation to witness great signs and wonders in the heavens and on the earth in the coming days. My experiences may seem too serious for some but they will challenge you to walk intimately with Jesus. I have escaped death many times and rescued in ways no man can take credit for, but God. We must work hard and endure all the obstacles to build good relationships within our families. Family is "blood thicker than water". We have a heritage and good inheritance to leave for our children's, children's children for a thousand generations. Our children and grand-children have the right to live in a good, healthy and blessed environment. We have an obligation to God and to our neighbour to share the Gospel of peace to birth souls into the kingdom. Such supernatural miracles are rarely noticed or acknowledged in the lives of ordinary people. The enemy is roaming, desperately trying to devour the weak and hypnotize the world with his deception. But God has a people He miraculously protects saves and hides for His glory. When God's favour rests on a life, every crooked path will be made straight and Jesus is exalted above all things. Surely goodness and mercy shall follow me all the days of my life; and I will dwell in the house of the Lord Forever. Psalms 23.6. The will of the Father is to draw all souls back into His kingdom where they belong.

Everyone who trusts in Jesus Christ for salvation is born again; they are the salt of the earth and light of the world. Matthew 5:13-14. As lights we expose darkness and as salt, we serve as preservatives, stopping the moral decay in our sin infested world. The baptism of the Holy Spirit and Fire will cause simple men, women and children to hunger for righteousness, discernment and godly wisdom, ready to do great exploits in the Kingdom. The resurrection power of Christ will be visible among commoners; on the streets, in villages and in the market place to display heaven's glory. Soon every form of evil will be destroyed. Men and women from cults and other faiths will be drawn to the Father's heart and set on fire with Christ's love. People will desire true fellowship with one another and share all things in common just like the first Church in the Book of Acts. Ready or not, "A Mantle of Elijah's Anointing plus Elisha's Anointing" is coming over the Church again. Wave after wave it will take hold of our sons and daughters who will do great exploits for the Kingdom. God fearing people will walk in this "Mantle" calling down fire, parting the oceans, raising the dead, cleansing lepers and birthing souls in multitudes. Young people will lead the older generation to live holy lives and out of the mouth of babes and nursing infants, we will hear the voice of God thunder. The earth and all in it shall tremble and worship God in reverential awe. The fiery eyes of Christ will set the nations ablaze with the fire of God. We will live to see it. O the glory of His presence like no other! Hallelujah!

Baptism of Fire and Burning

The Holy Spirit over took my life when I could barely think, walk, talk or dare to live another day. When I had no more strength to cry, He groaned from within. Tears became my food day and night but His joy

26

gave me strength to go on. Dragging myself off the soaking carpet I would simply bask in His presence desperately wanting Him to manifest Himself to me and in me. Suddenly I would feel a burning fire, electrifying my entire being. The Baptism of the Fire of the Holy Spirit will manifest the "Spirit of Burning;" which is a Spirit of sanctification. God used this process of "burning" to release me deeper in prayer and prophecy. He restored me in every area more than I could ever imagine. He carried me through some pretty nasty, ugly and painful situations. For with God nothing shall be impossible. Luke 1:37. It is only as we experience the fellowship of His sufferings that we will know Him and He will know us. Without a shadow of doubt I can say that I badly need God, I need the forgiveness and protection of the blood of Jesus and I need the Holy Spirit in my life. Without I would be in a psychiatric home as the devil wanted me confused and depressed. This choice is not easy but with God's grace we can do it. Only as we make the choice of taking the straight and narrow way of life, a life of nothing for me but all for thee, that we are conformed into the image of His Son. You too will hunger and thirst for intimacy with the Saviour. His passion and zeal will consume you right where you are and make you victorious in all things.

The same Holy Spirit is waiting to show up and show off Jesus to you in a whole new dimension, no man has yet seen or heard. The Lord wants to baptize you with His Holy Spirit and Fire to prepare you for something greater. Matthew 3:11-12. Apostle Paul declared with a deep cry...that I may know Him, and the power of His resurrection, and the fellowship of His sufferings, being made conformable unto His death. Philippians 3:10. Within the Spirit of Burning of the Holy Ghost will be a great impartation of His love in our hearts towards Him. We will meet Jesus in a great baptism of intimacy; so much so that within this union of love with our Lord, we can embrace the fires of suffering with joy. The Spirit of Burning also manifests in purging of the soul, bringing full repentance, and full spiritual transformation. This ministry of the Holy Spirit is necessary in one's life to prepare the Bride of Christ to be joined spiritually with the Lord our Bridegroom when He comes for the Church. Let us be glad and rejoice, and give honor to Him; for the marriage of the Lamb is come, and His wife hath made herself ready. And to her was granted that she should be arrayed in fine linen, clean and white. For the fine linen is the righteousness of the saints. Revelation 19:7. This righteousness can only come about through the baptism of fire.

No Holding Back

A life of continuous restoration, deliverance and healing is contagious; it will eventually show off the grace of a loving, forgiving, merciful Father. He will strip away your fears and clothe you in His garment of righteousness, peace and joy. Everywhere people are ready for a change of heart. Everyone is in need of a saving, loving, forgiving Father. All men, women and children are longing for pure love. When I share my stories, broken hearts are healed, lives are cleansed, the blind see, marriages restored, women feel whole again and captives are set free. People want to hear it all; the sad, bad and the ugly, hateful, fearful and wretched things we were delivered from. "If we ourselves were not there, we wouldn't have reached here. If we didn't pass through those dry, dreary and weary lands, we would not know how to handle the fullness and abundance of God in our lives." In humility together with Apostle Paul I too can say; I know how to be abased, and I know how to abound. Everywhere and in all things I have learned both to be full and to be hungry, both to abound and to suffer need. I can do all things through Christ who strengthens me. Philippians 4:12-13. There is no time to hold back any longer, to walk in shame, guilt or weakness. We are called to boldly rise up for the voiceless, the helpless and the needy. We have the authority to break off generational curses, traditions of our forefathers and establish the kingdom of Christ on earth. As kingdom royals we are ordained to live in the abundance of heaven. We are overcomers, more than conquerors called to sit in the heavenly places together with Jesus Christ. The fire of God is pure, lovely and good. It cannot be exchanged or replaced for anything in this whole wide world.

In this fast paced life, it is easy to ignore everyday living and forget to reflect on the blessings and goodness of God. He gave me a new song everyday to sing His praises in the sun, rain, snow and storm. I have learned that gratitude opens the doors to showers of blessings. Whatever the enemy meant for evil from the time of my birth, God in His supernatural power has turned it around for my good. As Joseph said to his brothers; But as for you, you meant evil against me; but God meant it for good... Genesis 50:20. Yes, All things work together for good to those who love God, to those who are the called according to His purpose. Romans 8:28. God wants to answer your heart's desire today. What He has done for me, He will do for you. I pray you too will testify of the goodness and faithfulness of God. I am fully persuaded that all good things come from the

Father of lights and all bad things come from the enemy. Satan is out to steal, kill and destroy all that is good, holy and beautiful but Jesus came to give us life and life more abundantly. John 10:10. Our purpose in life is to boast in our Lord.

The Holy Spirit is a breath away waiting to fulfill every promise in your life. Being confident of this very thing, that He who has begun a good work in me will complete it until the day of Jesus Christ. Philippians 1:6. It is no mistake that you are holding this book in your hands. God wants to make your joy complete. Together, let us carry the Fire of Christ's love to the nations so the world will see Jesus high and lifted up and His glory fire fill our temples. They will know us as one Body united in Christ's love. We are born for such a time as this to establish and manifest His kingdom on earth as it is in heaven.

Yielding to God is like a flower at dawn,
touched by the warmth of sun shine,
Swaying in the breeze and showing off beauty to the world,
Its perfume, for all to see what it is meant to be.

I am His beloved and He is mine!

I indeed baptize you with water unto repentance,
But He who is coming after me is mightier than I,
Whose sandals I am not worthy to carry.
He will baptize you with the Holy Spirit and fire.
His winnowing fan is in His hand,
And He will thoroughly clean out His threshing floor,
And gather His wheat into the barn;
But He will burn up the chaff with unquenchable fire.

Matthew 3:11-12

In The Midst Of It All

Blow after blow the angry waves beat
Against the sandy shores in the scorching heat
Each disappointment drives me to breaking point
In the midst of it all You never let me fall.

Like a roller coaster caught in its speed
Storms are raging, waters rise from the deep
Clouds gather, and day turns to night
In the midst of it all we see Your light.

Give us strength O Lord to endure
In fleshly temptations to seek you more
In victory and defeat not to let go
In the midst of it all, You we will call!

Angels ascending and descending so sweet
Holy Spirit in us Your fire released
Lost sheep come home, their wounds You will heal
In the midst of it all, Your blood was shed for all!

Chapter Two

Summer is one of the most special and exciting times of the year for many of us. We celebrate birthdays, anniversaries, engagements, weddings and outdoor barbecues, picnics with family and friends. This is a time we also share lots of memories. My dear mother started the birthdays on July 1st and a brother a week before mine. I met and married my late husband in July and we celebrated both our birthdays in the same month for twenty eight years. Two of our children were born days apart before our birthdays. July is a month of surprises, celebrations and gifts for the whole family. Memories are the key not to the past, but to the future. I know the experiences of my life will help you to face tomorrow. Healing is not the resolution of our past. It is the use of our past to draw us into a deeper relationship with God and to know His purpose for our lives. You too will learn to unpack your heart with words and to live in His joy!

Dead Blue Baby

July 18 1955, I was born in the third largest city formerly known as Calicut in South India, the third world. The umbilical cord was tightly wrapped around my neck and by a miracle I was made to live. This blue baby cheated death for the very first time. A fourth baby girl is superstitiously believed to be bad luck and I was reminded of it till I left home. My parents were battling with a sick child who died six months after my birth. So for many reasons I was the misfortunate child in the family. Mother confessed that I was an unwanted surprise and she tried to abort me through natural means. So early from the womb spirits of fear and rejection were transferred into my life. Besides my pretty face, curly hair and a cute smile, I had too many defects with my body and not very bright in school. Very tiny at birth, I was sickly with an extreme skin condition and struggled with wrinkled rough hands all of my life. By ten I was very self conscious and embarrassed trying to hide my old woman's hands, fumbling with words if someone looked them, worse of made fun of. I stood out skinny and tall everywhere, like the only 'long' girl in town with a long chin, dandy long legs and long neck. Teased and made fun of, they especially my older siblings called me many names to match all my imperfections. Meanwhile, I survived all these years with a lazy eye and a weak chest since birth. Sports were not my favourite but on the other hand I enjoyed drama, poetry and music. I learned to be a joker and laughed away all my flaws. I loved to entertain others, compose poetry and make speeches for every family occasion. Mother Superior Gabriel fancied training me in public speaking and singing on stage from a very early age. I was part of all the school plays, poetry elocution and singing contests from kindergarten to grade nine, until I switched schools in my senior year.

Bullying and Rejection

Unfortunately, they say teasing is often part of growing up. Almost every child experiences it to some extent. Teasing becomes bullying when it is repetitive or when there is a conscious intent to embarrass or hurt another child. I remember one evening taken to play with friends in the park. When we got there, my sister left me and ran to play with my friends. A neighbour's dog came charging from nowhere and gripped on to my skirt, biting me hard on the buttocks. I stood there crying and bleeding. The others laughed and kept on playing. I was embarrassed even more when in front of everyone I was forced to show my sister the dog bite on my bottom. Now that we are all grown, it's forgiven and I've learned to laugh it off. Like other incidents they too have become memories. The difference is they don't hurt anymore. Kids who face teasing or bullying feel rejected. They either become introverts or turn into bullies themselves. I turned into a hyper active tomboy. Sibling bullying can continue even as one gets older. When parents play favourites with their children it can trigger this unhealthy behaviour and lead to jealousy and strife. Many children even adults bully others to gain attention, to fit in a gang or to stand out in a group. This is peer-pressure and it is not healthy at all.

Rejection can be defined as the sense of being unwanted. This is an unloving spirit that can be passed down through the bloodline. Not only was I rejected from the womb, I was made to feel rejected. I was the black sheep of the family. I seemed to be doing everything wrong, got myself into a lot of trouble and punished or beaten with a cane. My parents played favourites with my older siblings. My older sister was more beautiful, with lovely smooth skin, fair in complexion and my younger siblings were too small. Because I was the hyperactive one, I was often sent out to the stores, meat market and did the odd chores; picking cow dung from the streets with my bare hands, drawing water from our well and help bring in the firewood. I turned everything into a fun thing. When I didn't know what to do I laughed and sang my way around. I openly suffered favouritism and comparison all my life. Being the middle child, with so many birth defects I always felt inadequate and neglected. As I grew older this spirit of rejection followed me and manifested in more ways you will learn in the stories I share. I married a foreigner to move far away from home. On purpose I married a 'black African' so that no one would take him from me (because he was 'black.' Later my mother rejected and mistreated my children the same way she did with me. Some of the nasty things I have done may have resulted from these bad experiences. Fortunately, every evil and bad in my life, God changed for my good and His glory.

When we are or made to feel rejected, we also reject ourselves. This lying spirit can cause you to feel sorry for yourself. It is the root of many emotional problems, health issues and depression. As a man thinks in his heart, so is he. Proverbs 23:7. We are called to kindness, to be hospitable and to lookout for one another. Thankfully I learned that as I grew older and became a Christian believer. A Christian home or any home must not tolerate bullying a spouse or a child. It may be hard but we must practice do unto others as you want done to you. Whatever you do, good or bad will always return one day to haunt you, so let us strive to do good. Jesus Himself suffered rejected and was abandoned by His own Father on the cross. Abba being a holy God could not look at His Son bearing the filthy sins of the whole world. The emotional wounds of our childhood are only healed when we know what God's Word says about us rather than what man says. When the devil shows up the next time, tell him; Jesus cares for you and you are His beloved forever. God gave me a special gift of love even before I knew Him as my Lord. He taught me to forgive unconditionally and to love without a reason.

Superstition and Witchcraft Stinks

Like most families we had it all; the generational baggage of curses, a history of superstitious beliefs, witchcraft, horoscope, fortune telling, tarot cards, palm reading, crystal ball gazers and more. But now we take authority in Jesus name and break the transfers and continue to pray, nullifying ancestral familiar spirits passed down. Early in the morning witches from the graveyard used to come house to house to tell people's fortune. In our desperation and ignorance we too visited witch doctors, conjurers and a tarot card reader. The more lies she told us the more we were drawn to listen. She must have cast a spell of magic on us. Once we went to a Hindu guru, the strangest, creepy creature I had ever seen. He was a midget, stunted body and long, very long braided hair that covered the whole yoga mat he sat on. He hardly spoke a word but people bowed before him and took the nasty ash and charms he gave them for luck. Later, I repented of these sins of witchcraft, pleaded forgiveness on behalf of all the family and received healing. Another word for superstition is "idolatry." It's based on blind faith; giving power to an object, person or rather believing they have magical powers. People still strongly believed in old wives tales and weird superstitious rituals and beliefs. There's a false interpretation for every sign, day, thing and creature. Even after all the modernization and enlightenment, superstitious beliefs persist in our societies today. In some cultures baby girls are aborted or killed after birth, women are burnt alive if they are barren or have physical defects. Some fear Friday the 13th, walking under a ladder, spilling salt, black cat crossing and wear good-luck charms for different ailments and reasons. All superstitious beliefs and witchcraft practices are a lie of Satan, who is against everything good and of God.

We prayed for and to the dead, even talked to evil spirits. An uncle had a spirit friend he shared cigars and liquor with, on the blade of his knife. By day break 'it' would disappear. People still communicate with deceased relatives or spirit guides. These are familiar spirits. Demons are used by a medium or witch to deceive others. Often, familiar spirits are tied to you and your family by bloodline from generations and try to use the form of a loved one to deceive. Our prayers have no bearing on someone once they are dead. One's eternal destiny is confirmed at the time of death. Either they are saved through faith in Jesus Christ and are in heaven or they are forever tormented in hell. Regard not them that have familiar spirits, neither seek after wizards, to be defiled by them: I am the LORD your God.

Leviticus 19:31, Deuteronomy 18:11. Jesus used the story of the rich man and Lazarus the beggar to teach us that the unrighteous are eternally separated from God. Luke 16:19-31. They will remember they rejected the gospel of truth and cannot be remedied once in hell.

Many of us love to hear and tell scary ghost stories and then scream in the dark, fear to be alone and can't sleep at night. Still some fear of being in the dark. No wonder! Did this ever happen to you? We read our week-ly horoscope and believed in it. Even now people do these things. They watch scary movies, play dangerous demonic games, dress their little kids for Halloween and indulge in ungodly satanic rituals either knowingly or unknowingly. It may be fun for a time but no fun to the devil. You open doors for satanic attack and create spiritual strongholds. Strongholds are patterns of thinking built upon lies; brick upon brick, deception and error passed down from generation to generation. Even Christians can be op-pressed by evil spirits. For the weapons of our warfare are not carnal but mighty in God for pulling down strongholds, casting down arguments and every high thing that exalts itself against the knowledge of God, bringing every thought into captivity to the obedience of Christ. 2 Corinthians 10:3-5. The spooky pictures of the devil are unreal. He has no horns, no tail and is not black. The Bibles says Lucifer was a one of the most beautiful archangels created by God. He is one of God's creations, a wor-ship leader from the start with music in his being. After he was filled with pride and jealousy he rebelled against God and became a fallen angel and took a third of the angels who rebelled with him. Read Ezekiel 28. This is more reason to expose Satan, so God's people can know the truth and the truth will set them free, like it did you and me.

The Anglo Indian Community

We are a mixed race mostly of British and Portuguese descent. Eng-lish educated and entirely European in our habits, dress and language, we were more "Anglo" than "Indian". Most of our customs, traditions and even mother-tongue is English. We have a mixture of Western and Indian names. Many are Anglicans and Catholics but have never read the Bible until recently. We religiously followed all the rituals and feasts of the Church. Anglo-Indians ran the railways, post and telegraph, customs, tea, coffee and tobacco plantations, the coal and gold fields. They were the best teachers, nurses, secretaries and doctors.

Our mothers made the best Christmas cakes and every family had their own secret recipe handed down from our grandparents. Besides being a fun-loving lot we also picked up other negative habits and traits from our forefathers. They love fashion, merrymaking and socializing. The community is now disappearing as people have found new lives and merged into the mainstream. Most of our children are born abroad and their connection to this community is very fragile, some are completely disconnected. We ourselves have migrated to foreign lands and may be the last Anglo-Indian generation alive. I am glad to be part of a culture known for its good cheer, generous hospitality and friendship. Grateful that I was born, grew up and lived in a country like India with its enormous diversity of people, languages, foods, religions and traditions that has helped me to become a people person now.

Religion vs. Relationship

Human beings are born from intimacy, created with love for the purpose to love. Relationship is in the very core of our being. We hunger for love from the moment we are conceived in our mother's womb. Children never want to be separated from their parents. "Christianity is not a religion; it's a relationship with Jesus Christ." God's amazing Love and Grace paid the price for our sins when Jesus died on that old rugged tree (cross). There are a lot of "religions" in the world that has nothing to do with God and many people in "religion" who will never make it to Heaven. Religion is man-made based on trying to get to God through rules, regulations and works. I've been there and done that, faithfully followed every ritual of the Catholic faith and prayed every printed prayer in the book. But my peace and joy only came from walking in a love relationship with The Father, Jesus The Son and The Holy Spirit. I have nothing against Catholic people or those of other faiths but against the deception of the enemy that has messed up too many lives. Satan deceives man with control and spiritual blindness. Most of my family, friends and the folk I know and love are good Catholics, Hindus, Buddhists, Muslims, some Atheists and Christians of many denominations. But I believe that now, your heart too is crying out for unconditional love and to know the truth about Jesus who bled, died and forever lives to daily intercede for you and me. That Christ may dwell in your hearts by faith; that you, be rooted and grounded in love, may be able to comprehend with all the saints what is the width and length and depth and height - to know the love of Christ which passes knowledge…. Ephesians 3:17-21. I pray you will receive this pure, amazing love and know that Jesus loves you!

Like good Catholics, we too visited shrines, churches and temples searching for answers. Our parents often took us to visit Mary's shrine in South India almost every year. We took a train, rented a motel and paid our vows. This was hypocrisy! Even there my father was drunk and misbehaved. It was an outward show and not a matter of the heart. We faithfully worshiped in Infant Jesus Church and saw crowds of Hindus and Muslims flock there to burn candles and bring flowers to pay vows for their desperate needs. Such religious rituals have no meaning or satisfaction in life without the Holy Spirit. I had gone to the shine in Velankanni even on my own and from the entrance of the Church to the front of the altar I scraped my knees and lit candles to Mary. This was ignorance and simply mocking our living God who commanded us to worship NO other god but Jesus Christ the risen Lord. It is idolatry in the clearest form. We honour, and love Mary as the earthly mother of Jesus on earth but we should not, cannot worship her. Mary is not God and her exaltation in the Catholic Church has no foundation in Scripture. While we may and should appreciate the ministry of men and women, they are only instruments used as vessels for the glory of God. Christ alone is our mediator. Paul clearly points this out in scripture. Mary herself would agree because she knew well more than anyone else, that the Child she gave birth to was to become the Saviour of mankind - including her·own Saviour. She too was in that upper room waiting along with the one hundred and twenty disciples and then filled with tongues of fire on the day of Pentecost.

Alcohol Destroys Families

As children we endured much shame and fear living with an alcoholic father. Christmas holidays were the worst; because when everyone else is having a jolly good time my father was drunk causing a commotion. He would become violently abusive, cursing my mother and threatening us with his filthy mouth. From young I remember his sudden outburst of anger and screams, and he was only getting worse. He was a jolly good man without the drink, helping others and loving to his family. I loved my father very much but never liked his drinking habit and dirty mouth. When we saw him staggering from afar we always prepared for the worst. He was unpredictable. Strange enough he was different with friends and outsiders. When he was sober he would pretend like nothing ever happened. Nights I would lie awake with fear and jump up to the slightest sound and to my mother's screams. That was dreadful horrible for a child. He chased us around with a hockey stick swearing like a madman. We stayed with our neighbours for nights and prayed he sober up by the morning. Imagine one New Years Eve we ended up in the railway hospital. My mother was badly beaten and bleeding in one eye. I walked up and down the whole day comforting her, trying to convince my father and helping my younger siblings. By the time I graduated, my mother was fed up of the abuse. I had no idea how much she instigated it all. But I couldn't take it as much as she did. We dreaded for our lives and had no other choice but to leave and start our own lives.

Several years later, my father met with a serious railway accident and lost his leg. He was drunk coming home in his own carriage and jumped of the wrong side of the railway tracks while the train was moving. He must have done this many times before but this time he fell in between and knee down his leg was severed immediately. Alcohol is an evil 'spirit', a demonic mocker of everything good. It starts as fun and then ruins everything and everyone. It ruins families. Drunkenness can cause the nicest person to be a fool. When people are drunk, they try to get away with anything; incest, adultery, perversion and abuse. It brings great fear and insecurity to the whole household. Alcohol causes early deaths, disease, and rips families apart. Any addiction regardless of ethnicity or social group, rich or poor, destroys marriages and lives. Unless you begin to hate your lifestyle, sin and unclean habits you cannot be free. Sadly two of my brothers turned into alcoholics and died young. The older had a severe lung infection with holes. Even though he was born again and changed his lifestyle, he suffered the consequences till his death. The younger brother was an addict and hanged himself under the influence of liquor. After witnessing so many tragedies and heartaches caused by this disease, I don't wish any child, man or woman to suffer from this or any addiction. Even though I had an inclination to behave like my parents, the Lord supernaturally snatched me right out in time and changed my whole direction. Now, it is my responsibility to warn others. We must not put our children through such danger, to endure the things we suffered as kids. We must forgive our mothers and fathers regardless of what they have done to us because the Bibles tells us so. As kids they too may have suffered and had no good examples to follow. Why 'hurting people hurt other people.' It's not going to be easy but we realize that forgiveness gives us peace of mind and it will release healing. We have the power to forgive, break such ancestral curses and choose to live life differently.

I made an effort to visit my father as often as I could in Erode. But after a few drinks he would repeat his old stories and get all upset. It's sad some men fail to stand up and take responsibility as fathers, especially towards their girls and young daughters. Notice most evil spirits manifest at night and in this case after two or more drinks. When he got abusive and threatening, I had to run out of the house even if it's very late at night. Once I ran to take a train, the station was only minutes away so I hurriedly walked in the dark. On my way, I was stopped by a family friend whom I hoped would help me get a train reservation. (That's what most railway folks do, help others). To make a long story short, he abused my trust, sexually assaulted me with lying and false promises. Like most teenage girls, I blamed myself for the incident. When I tried to tell my mother the next day, she refused to listen and ignored me. After a few days the man shows up in our house. The most shocking thing I came to understand later was that he was also my mother's boyfriend. This shattered me to pieces. When a young girl is insecure and not safe with her own parents whom does she trust? Many such and even worse cases happen today. Children and teenagers suffer terrible things when a home is broken, which is unfair. We could not express our feelings back then no matter what happened in our house or lives. Our parents were supposedly strict and we couldn't go to them freely like our children come to us today. There was too much pretense, and religion helped cover up all the dirty laundry. The word 'sex' was sacrilegious to even mention. I've learned that communication is the key to any relationship, especially in a marriage and with children. I've used this tool too often and it works. It has helped me succeed in many ways. Silence is not always golden; it can cause frustration and sometimes early death.

After this incident and many other embarrassing ones that followed, I had no strength to live and tried to commit suicide. I swallowed a bunch of straight pins in desperation, started smoking my mother's filter-less cigarettes and hated being a girl. July 18th 1973 when I turned eighteen, I was drunk the whole day not able to move. I emptied a whole bottle of rum which I usually hate and did not want to wake up. It was a miracle that not one of those pins affected me. Such bitter experiences filled my heart with hatred for men; I detested every man on the planet and wanted to hurt them bad. I tried to confide with a relative but she too brushed me aside saying 'that's your problem!' She got involved with the same guy and everything got messy. They were making out in front of me and laughed at my plight while I wanted to die! Today the coin has changed after decades God has me on the victory side and sadly they were not able to keep their marriage or children from repeating those same old curses of horror till this day. I wanted to punish myself, I didn't know what I wanted but it was ugly. This is exactly how so many females feel today and yes God fights for the innocent. He protected me in mysterious ways and continues to do so even after all these many years. Each time something bad showed up, He sent strangers, His angels to rescue me. Angels would supernaturally snatch me out in time. How do I know this? I'd never seen them before, could not trace where they came from and where they had gone. When I was hurting God was watching; when I was helpless He saw my pain and miraculously healed me again and again. The Holy Spirit showed me a secret in forgiveness and I couldn't trade that for the world. I was determined to do things differently than my parents and siblings and the Lord moved in my favour. Whatever the case may be, trust Him today. Only He can turn 'your mess into a message, mistakes into miracles and exchange your hurts for halos and scars for stars.' He will give you peace.

Witchcraft is Rebellion

Eight long years and after several attempts to reconcile my parents, a friend introduced me to a witch doctor. I was tired of the blame for all the mishaps in our family. This was the first time I got involved in black magic for myself. Then, I didn't know about witches or how dangerous witchcraft was. This crystal ball gazer was an Anglo-India witch. His house was dark, full of skulls, crystal balls, weird objects and statues of all sorts including Mary. He even prayed and kissed the statues before he started. At this time I was still a Catholic. I paid him a lot of money. He gave me an ink to write to my father and the strangest thing, the magic worked! My letter found my father sick, weak and lonely. After seven days a friend admitted him in hospital close to where we lived. When I got the news I was excited to bring him home. It was not an easy process, because he still cursed and screamed but we finally got him to agree to live with us. He was too weak to put up a fight. My parents were reunited! Later I repented of my sin of witchcraft and magic. Months before his death for the first and the last time in my entire life, my dad put his arms around my shoulder and talked about my future. We celebrated his birthday in November and the following year on April 13th on Good Friday he quietly passed away. As we were laughing and chatting away by his hospital bed, he fell into my arms and in seconds was gone. I grieved my father's death for a long time.

Witchcraft is an act of the devil which not only manipulates the minds of people, but it can wreak a life physically, emotionally and spiritually. For rebellion is as the sin of witchcraft... 1 Samuel 15:23. Many Christians are ignorant about the devil's schemes. John 10:10. On the contrary, to remain ignorant of who Satan is, and how he operates is dangerous. Be sober (be serious minded) and vigilant for your adversary the Devil walks about like a roaring lion, seeking whom he may devour. 1 Peter 5:8. Ignorance is foolishness for it can lead to your destruction. Unless we learn about our enemy we cannot protect our households from the dangers of his traps. Know about the devil and his evil because he knows you too well. We must learn how to pray against evil, declare God's will and purpose for our lives. But knowing Jesus in an intimate relationship will destroy the works of all darkness and prepare us for victory in the Kingdom of God.

Deliverance from Fear

In prayer one day, the Holy Spirit showed me different areas of my life that needed healing. Besides being rejected from the womb, I also had fear. Fear is the first negative emotion we learn as children. ALL form of fear is of the enemy. When a spirit of fear takes root in a life, we become slaves to it. Faith brings freedom, fear controls and puts one in bondage. The Lord took me through several incidents in my life; when I was three, through my teens, as a young adult and in my older years. Through the process I felt so much pain and fear inside of me. I repented for holding on to those fears, renounced them, forgave everyone involved whether they are living or dead and received my deliverance. The heaviness was unbearable and I began to weep and weep until I felt a release of His love, peace and joy. I confessed each situation and it seemed like something was torn away from me but I felt great peace. God is our healer. Even Jesus had fear in the garden before He suffered death and sweated blood but angels came and strengthened Him. My fears did not go away all at once. As I meditated on the Word of God and received the love of my heavenly Father He made me stronger and bolder each day. Perfect love casts out fear, for fear has torment. I John 4:18. It is the enemy's bait to silence you, to keep you blind and bound.

Fear causes: repeated illnesses, allergies, colds, pride, substance abuse and every abuse, headaches, miscarriages, divorces, negative reactions and more. Satan has phobia in all things concerning you, so he attacks you first with his lies. Even his own shadow scares him. Yet we who abide in the Secret Place will not be shaken. Psalm 91. We must be strong as lions and defeat him with the blood of Jesus and the Word of our testimony. Fear not but have faith in God!

Killed in an Accident

Busy with college, work and life, I was also trying out acting and modeling. One evening, I was returning from a modeling event and a huge truck suddenly lost control and came head on into our motorcycle. I heard a loud crash and lost consciousness. The rider of the motorcycle was in a serious condition, crushed under his bike but I was found lying way across the opposite side of the road. Thinking I too was dead, they quickly threw our bodies on the back of a police car and rushed to the nearest hospital. The next day newspapers reported details of the accident; "Rider and Passenger Dead!" There was no recognition of the vehicle, it was completely crushed. I believe, if I had not been thrown off that bike I too would have being instantly killed. The next day my friends came with flowers to mourn my death. Once again I miraculously 'cheated death!' I survived with multiple fractures below the hip and on my thigh. I was bleeding from severe cuts and bruises on my head, hands and body. My femur was fractured completely through the bone and I was in excruciating pain. Because of the pain I could not allow anyone to touch me. Carefully trying to hold the separated pieces of bone in my hand they wheeled me to the operation theater. The hospital shook with my loudest screams. The staff and patients became my friends, including the doctors and a police chief who later helped me fight a court case in my favour. The orthopedic surgeons carried out a procedure to join the broken fractures with a twelve inch metal rod; that was drilled through my hip down to the thigh. After the surgery both my legs especially the broke one was swollen three times the size. I would need several months to recover and then transferred to the rehabilitation center. They said, I had to heal from the shock, surgery and learn to walk on crutches. If I did recover completely I would have a permanent limp for the rest of my life. I suffered unbearable pain and could not move, lying on my back for weeks with weights hanging down my foot. Every day visitors came to cheer me up.

Family and close friends knew that I lived a hectic, wild teenage life. Some felt sorry for my condition while others scoffed and laughed because I lay helpless. A cousin, like a big brother to me came to visit with his wife. He was just saved and changed his life style from being a hypnotist and magician to serving Jesus Christ. Before they left he prayed that 'I would rise up and walk normal again in Jesus' name.' I didn't think he was serious. Like Sarah laughed because she was too old to conceive, I too laughed and mocked him. This was during the Easter week. In a few days, I was beginning to heal. The weights were taken off; still the bruises and scars were very sore, my feet were weak and I could barely stand. Gradually the muscle and strength was coming back into my body and the doctors were amazed with my speedy recovery. By now I was beginning to move a little bit. Soon I was discharged to go home. With oil massages, basking in the sun and painful exercises I got better each day. I taught myself to stand up and take baby steps with the help of a cane. I was determined to walk again. Severe pain from the surgery and the metal rod in my thigh but I slowly began to actually walk. The more people felt sorry for me and said unkind things, the harder I tried. Every step was a big achievement. With the help of a hired cycle rickshaw (a carriage pulled with a bicycle) I went to work. Every day I climbed a small stairway to my seat in the office and it felt great. Until one suffers the need for a part of the body we have no idea what it feels like. In pain I practiced standing, walking and climbing stairs until I needed the cane no longer. I was invited to the May Queen Ball that year and won the 'Midimix Queen'. This dance was sponsored by an 'herbal soap' company in India, which is still in the market today. Two years later the metal rod was removed from my body and today am leaping, jumping and praising God.

Healing is Children's Bread

Yes, I believe it was God who healed me! He used people, practicing doctors but the blood of Jesus was shed to complete my healing. In normal circumstances it would have taken much longer but God is not restricted with time. When my cousin prayed I believe God was merciful. Even though my mouth did not agree with him and I doubted, He touched my heart to receive healing from the inside out. Healing is the children's bread. Mark 7:27. It's our portion as children of God. The Lord's Prayer tells us to ask for our daily bread. Bread is a symbol of food, nourishment, health and strength. On the cross Jesus not only paid for the forgiveness of our sins but also for our healing. "By His stripes, we were (already) healed." 1 Peter 2:24. I am a witness of the healing power of a living God. Without the bleeding nail pierced hands of God, I wouldn't be alive today to tell you this story. I can testify that each one of my miracles were nothing short of the supernatural. Not that I have reached perfection yet. Healing can happen instantly or gradually. Jesus went about healing all who were sick and oppressed by the devil. Matthew 12:15. Every day I confess my healing in my body, mind and soul. Healing is for today. Healing is for everyone. I believe in miracles and I believe in a healing Jesus!

Forgiveness and Repentance

Love for hurtful parents or persons don't come from our own abilities. It comes from the supernatural love of Jesus who died for us even while we were yet undeserving sinners. Romans 5:8. We must honour our mother and our father not because they deserve it but because God commanded us to do so. And they sacrificially brought us into this world out of love no matter what their failures and short-comings were. The least we can afford to give our parents in return is 'honour.' Whether they are living or dead we can choose to forgive. Forgiveness and repentance go together. To be forgiven, we must forgive others. Jesus taught us to pray in Matthew 6:12 ...forgive us our sins, as we forgive those who sinned against us. Living with unforgiveness can cause mental agony and (even) lead to physical illness. When we are wronged by others, the hurt that we feel inside can quickly turn into lasting resentment, bitterness and anger. If we confess our sins, He is faithful and just to forgive us our sins and to cleanse us from all unrighteousness. 1 John 1:9. Forgiveness releases us to live our lives, to let go of the past and learn to love like Jesus. Repentance helps us to turn away and trust in God's grace every day. Never be ashamed that you need help, or forgiveness.

Let us pray:

O Righteous Heavenly Father, I come to You in the name of Jesus Christ. I accept You today as my Saviour and Lord over all things. I ask Your forgiveness of all my sins that are many, the things that I have done and failed to do. With my own free will I forgive my father, mother, my siblings and all those who have used, abused, rejected, hurt, wounded or failed to love me. I repent and renounce every wicked thought, deed or word. I cancel every argument against me and pull down strongholds in Jesus name. I take authority and break ancestral curses, hereditary spirits and soul ties off my life from both sides of my bloodline going back four generations way down to a thousand generations. I apply the precious blood of Jesus and ask You sanctify me and my household. Fill me now Holy Spirit with Your power, love and a sound, disciplined mind. I praise and thank You for what You've done, are doing, and will do in my life for Your glory. Change my heart to love You more and keep me forever sealed for Your name sake. Make me the man/woman you have destined me to be. I pray this in agreement with all the family of God, receiving our complete healing, deliverance and restoration according to Your will. Thank You Master, we receive Your righteousness, peace and joy in the Holy Spirit in all situations. We pray this in the mighty, matchless name of Jesus! Amen.

For You formed my inward parts;
You covered me in my mother's womb.
I will praise You, for I am fearfully and wonderfully made;
Marvelous are Your works, and that my soul knows very well.
My frame was not hidden from You, when I was made in secret,
And skillfully wrought in the lowest parts of the earth.
Your eyes saw my substance, being yet unformed.
And in Your book they all were written,
The days fashioned for me, when as yet there were none of them.
How precious also are Your thoughts to me, O God!
How great is the sum of them!
If I should count them, they would be more in number than the sand;
When I awake, I am still with You.

Psalm 139:13-16

Mistakes into Miracles

If I was not born, there'll be no stories to tell
A soul breathed from heaven, singing spring up O well.
Watching nights turn to day from bitter to sweet,
Horrors become halos and defeat to dreams.

He gives sun and rain to the good and the bad
Causing His face to shine to make our hearts glad.
Loving is not easy, but it's worth it to show
Jesus died for the world, especially for those who are sore.

He makes scars shine like stars and tears into pearls
The impossible He makes possible and obstacles are stepping stones.
Darkness is exposed, fear cannot stay
His light shines brighter; Faith will make the way.

Forgiveness is the secret; love sets you free
Living becomes easy, because Jesus died for you and me
Prayers become incense, sweet and so true
God changes mistakes into miracles, so you can smile too.

My family, First Holy Communion and in my teens

Modeling, School Play and Midimix Queen

Chapter 3

Pen pals are not common today, but they were our hobbies in the 1960's and 1970's. Letter writing was my favourite, way I could express and share my thoughts and feelings with others. Like the actual writing with a pen and paper, before emails, cell phones or internet was ever thought of. My pen pals were girls and boys from all across India and a few abroad; Japan, England and Africa. We exchanged letters, shared stories, photographs, greeting cards and gifts. Those early days were simple when we actually used nib pens, dipped in a bottle of ink and used blotting paper. We wrote sweet nothings, about hobbies, birthdays, school stuff, just making new friends! I waited for the mailman every day because I knew he had something for me. Just recently I was able to reconnect with an old pen pal after 47 years. We started as teenagers writing letters to each other from two different cities in India. Interestingly now we are grandmothers living in different parts of the world. Our older siblings connected us when they were friends at that time. We are now catching up via email and hoping to meet someday.

African students toured the country and neighbouring Colombo in Sri Lanka, (formerly known as Ceylon) during the summer holidays. The garden city of Bangalore was one of their favourite spots. This was a safe cosmopolitan city; known for its great weather, beautiful gardens, friendly people and tourism. The streets were not crowded like now. I used to ride my bike to college and work but today a lot has changed. Bangalore is called 'the Silicon Valley of India', a nickname for its status as a hub for information technology (IT) and attracts job opportunities and more international students. A colleague of mine used to bring African students to our house from time to time. They were friendly, mannerly and intelligent and we liked them. To live in India one has to be smart and hard working. India may be a free country in many ways but they still cannot escape racism. Hopefully that is slowly changing. Skin colour didn't bother me because India has a lot of dark-skinned people and they discriminate even among themselves. Today students come from all over the world and some of the churches I know are flooded with African students. Our house guest was friends with a boy named John from Uganda. She moved on, got married but his letters were still coming. I replied to one of them and realized that John's friend Apollo was studying in India. Appy Nyabagwe (that was his African clan name) and I became pen pals. Apollo was a university student in a town close to New Delhi, the capital city of India when I was graduating from College. Though we were different in many ways, we had a lot in common. I used to entertain my father with letters and photographs of my friends months before he passed away. My family knew all about the only African pen pal I had for over a year. After the loss of my father, Apollo comforted me with sympathy cards and notes to cheer me up. We became close friends.

When my mother and sister went shopping one evening, they saw a huge Hindu procession with crowds of people beating their drums, singing and dancing on the streets. This is a usual sight in the free country of India. To their surprise in the middle of the crowd was an auto rickshaw (today called baby taxis) with an African gentleman looking for directions. He stopped the vehicle and gave them a piece of paper with my address written on it. Familiar with his name, my mother brought him home to wait for me. This was hilarious! Before I got in the door, my sister met me giggling and said I had a visitor. I was shocked to see Apollo sitting in my father's reclining canvas chair. He was grinning from ear to ear. I couldn't contain my excitement and just froze. He stood up, nodded his head and greeted me. We had no home telephone and the only means of communication was by regular mail or a telegram. He was touring Sri Lanka and Bangalore and decided to surprise me to express his condolences in person. Repeatedly he said he was sorry for my loss, with a sad funny face that made me burst out laughing. We chatted for a while and went out for dinner. Not sure if I should call this a date but it was not usual for Indian girls to date black Africans in those days. Apollo and I connected right away; nothing mattered at this point. I got out of my yellow printed sari and jumped into jeans. This was the best day of my entire life. I was on top of the moon. His gentle, compassionate love swept me off my feet and I was beginning to like his company. We spent the next few days feasting on cherry Jello and whipped cream on Mahatma Gandhi road (MG), sightseeing the beautiful LalBagh Botanical Gardens, Cuban Park and the Vidhana Soudha which is the largest Legislative building in Bangalore in the whole State of Karnataka. We had no television sets back then so we watched a comedy in Rex Theater, on Bangalore's famous Brigade road.

One year my family went to visit my sister for her birthday in the Indian French city of Pondicherry. Known as Puducherry district today, it is situated south of Chennai. This is one of the most popular tourist destinations. People came from all over the world to enjoy its extraordinary charm. This city was under French rule until 1954 and some people here still speak French and English with a French accent. We lodged in the inn of a mixed African and Indian couple close to the main hospital where my sister trained. This was the first time I met a black African grown man in the 1960's living in India. If am not mistaken, he was a Ghanaian from West Africa who settled in India after he married. They had a gorgeous daughter with beautiful curly hair and she was a doctor working in the hospital nearby. These folks were jovial, friendly and fun loving. My parents hit it off with them right away. It was just around Christmas time; we sang carols in their bar and had a jolly good time. We didn't see them again. I never dreamed almost twenty years later I would have a coloured family of my own.

First African Indian Marriage

In the East African tradition, a marriage proposal is an event of celebration and gifts. The boys' relatives would come to the house of the bride-to-be to speak on his behalf. The gifts can vary from cows, goats, property, etc. Because of our British roots, Anglo-Indians never followed the Indian customs. Love marriage was acceptable within India and preferably to whites but was not common with black Africans. I was one of the first Anglo-Indian girls to break the colour barrier in Bangalore. Apollo was the youngest of 15 siblings who were all in Uganda so his closest friend acted as his spokesman. This was amusing! He wanted me to accompany him back to Uganda after his graduation, but we first had to be married. We began to make plans for the wedding and organize our travel to Africa. My family was happy for us and joined in our plans. The Catholic Church refused to marry us not for any other reason, but because he was an African student.

This was the first time I had ever experienced racial discrimination. I was a practicing Roman Catholic but Apollo was an atheist. He had Protestant roots but did not believe in anything. He searched for truth everywhere, visited Hindu temples, Mosques and different Churches but found no peace. He concluded 'God is dead' and posted a big sign in his dorm room. A Catholic Priest from the Sacred Heart Church in our neighbouring town was familiar with Africans in Kenya and agreed to perform our marriage ceremony. In a week Apollo converted into a Roman Catholic, received all the sacraments of the faith and we got married on July 23rd 1979. My oldest brother walked me down the aisle, and my younger siblings were my bridesmaid and groomsman. It was the smallest wedding with close family and friends but this was the best of all my sweet memories. I was excited to be married and was soon going to travel out of India for the very first time.

Interracial marriages were rare in India then. Most probably, I was the first Indian to marry a black African Ugandan in the whole of South India. Some girls had affairs with Nigerian students who abandoned them when they got pregnant. Because of this behaviour people disliked all Africans. Relatives, including my family gave us a trial span of one to two years. Racism is embarrassing, shameful and must not be tolerated anywhere no matter the colour of your skin. We became a spectacle. Anywhere we went, shopping or just for walks people stared, made rude remarks and laughed. An old aunt of mine teased saying I would get "tar-ball babies". In crowds, airports, church and on the streets in India and in Uganda our family stood out. Still this didn't bother us. Instead we felt unique and special. We were the first Interracial Marriage, African family in our Full Gospel Church in Manama Bahrain. We were loved by the family of God. Today, there are many mixed families in India, Uganda and Bahrain. We saw racial discrimination and skeptics in and outside India. We were denied, delayed, turned down, rejected and humiliated because of the outward appearance of our skin colour. What a shame! In India relatives ignored my husband when they came to visit. But not long after, one of them started a church and most of his congregations now are black African students. In Uganda some were against Indians. Friends and distant relatives sent rude messages to the family. While we visited the Country once, we got a big bag of red chilies as an insult. Certain people, supposedly well educated and fluent in English, purposely spoke in their mother tongue when I was around. One of the girls began to sing spiritual songs and tried to flirt with my husband each time she saw me.

Funny thing, I started to laugh and sing along. But not too long after did the tables turn and I am alive today to see the glory of God in our lives. Too many stories along the way have proved how God fights for His own children. He has given me grace to forgive and to love them anyway. To be oppressed, helpless and lonely in a foreign country is the worst one can ever endure. I persevered! For whatever reasons these biases were displayed, in ignorance or stupidity and however painful they were, as a couple we overcame. It was our determination to stand against all odds and show others that any marriage can work. When God puts even inter-racial marriages together nothing can separate us.

On the positive side, we were able to relate to people from diverse backgrounds. When we got saved as 'Born Again Believers,' the plan of God began to unfold in our favour. Being victims of racism, discrimination and loneliness we were able to make others feel special. Our children attracted smiles and sparked off conversations with anyone; in the plane, elevators, airports, parks, churches and the market places. Families and single moms were able to open their wounds, talk about their situations and receive healing. Through the years of trials and challenges the Lord rewarded us with a rich and lasting relationship for almost twenty nine years. We had four beautiful coloured children and lots of gorgeous grandchildren with curly black hair. The Holy Spirit brought the reality of heaven into our lives through each and every circumstance. God made it possible. Love made our marriage work even in the midst of obstacles. There are different races and colours in this world because God made them that way. So we can unite, complement each other and celebrate our differences. Together, we represent heaven on earth. We represent God! Our God is Love!

Colour Is Skin Deep

As long as we live in this flesh we must fight the good fight of faith against cultural and racial discrimination if we desire a society of peace. These differences are real, but should not be the cause for prejudice - pre-judging someone before you know them. Every person harbors some amount of bias on a number of things including race. Most of these biases are the result of ignorance and fear; fear of the unknown. It is purely emotional. When people feel insecure, they don't know how to react. Having a cultural bias doesn't mean one is a racist. Because of colonization from the British Empire Indians tend to behave like their former masters. They discriminate among themselves and advertise for 'fairer' brides for their sons. In some customs, the dowry (bride price) may even depend on the colour of the girl's skin because they want grandchildren with lighter skin. This is ridiculous and an unfair practice but it is there all the same! Many have traveled abroad and are highly educated but still are uncomfortable with interracial marriages and struggle with skin colour. All people are beautiful and intelligent. Colour is only skin deep. Even in heaven there is diversity of tribes, tongues and peoples of many nations, BUT all are worshipping God in one accord. Then I saw another angel flying in the midst of heaven, having the everlasting gospel to preach to those who dwell on the earth—to every nation, tribe, tongue, and people — saying with a loud voice, "Fear God and give glory to Him, for the hour of His judgment has come; and worship Him who made heaven and earth, the sea and springs of water." Revelation 14:6-7. We are living in an age where there's diversity practically everywhere we turn but how we appreciate it and enjoy the difference is what matters.

One's idea of compatibility should be based on the facts of a situation not on the color of the people. There are same-race couples that are less compatible than interracial couples, because the issue is not race, not even colour but sufficient spiritual union, common conviction, and similar expectations to make the marriage workable. The only marriage constraints put on a Christian is they marry the opposite sex and they marry another Believer in Jesus Christ. One Corinthians 7:39 and two Corinthians 6:14. There is too much pain, hurt and selfishness in this world already so it's time we do something. We must overcome fear, and learn how to liberate people from the continuing bondage of poverty, deprivation, suffering, gender and other discriminations. Be proud of who you are. There is no difference in Christ Jesus. God broke all differences by pouring out His Holy Spirit on ALL flesh. And it shall come to pass in the last days, says God, that I will pour out of My Spirit on all flesh; your sons and your daughters shall prophesy, your young men shall see visions, your old men shall dream dreams. And on My menservants and on My maidservants I will pour out My Spirit in those days; And they shall prophesy. Act 2:17-18. We are all made different and special with a specific purpose to enjoy life and to celebrate one another on planet earth we temporarily call home.

Before we took off to Uganda we spent a few weeks in Aligarh in Uttar Pradesh. We met other mixed couples and International students from different parts of Africa and from other nations. We cooked buffalo meat, mixed Indian and African dishes on a small oil stove in our one room apartment. People were curious about our relationship and invited us everywhere. The only transportation in this small town to the local bus station was a Tonga (carriage pulled by two cows), swaying from side to side on bumpy roads. Every weekend we took a two hour bus ride to New Delhi for some city life. In the restaurants people stopped eating and would turn around to look at us like we were their amusement. We learned to laugh about it by now and Apollo babbled a few words in Hindi to send them away. This was my first visit to North India so we toured New Delhi and Old Delhi. There is little difference between Old and New Delhi, located on the banks of River Yamuna. New Delhi is the capital city of India, the seat of the Indian government and is part of the large city of Old Delhi. The streets and lanes in New Delhi are beautiful and tidy when compared with those of Delhi, with older buildings and old monuments. The towering archway of India Gate is at the center of New Delhi. It is a war memorial built in memory of the Indian soldiers who lost their lives fighting for the British Army in World War I. At night the whole building glowed under floodlights.

We journeyed to East Africa in October of 1979 making a transit in Kenya to spend time with relatives. Nairobi is the most dynamic and largest city in Kenya, also known as the 'green city in the sun'. The weather was extremely superb. We enjoyed sightseeing beautiful gardens and Nairobi's biggest and oldest National Park. The only National park in the world that is less than ten kilometers away from the Nairobi's city centre with only a fence separating the park from Kenya's capital. This is home to black rhinos, lions, leopards, cheetahs, hyenas, buffalos, giraffes, zebras, wildebeests, elands, hippos and more than 400 species of all kinds of birds. Each sight was more fascinating than the other. We went to the elephant and rhino orphanage and the only giraffe breeding center in East Africa. We walked through forests, safari trails and along the River to see hippos, crocodiles and all different kinds of baboons and monkeys. Some mischievous long- tailed, small-faced monkeys followed us, trying to snatch anything they can get a hold of. They travel in groups carrying babies on their backs, jumping from tree to tree. We gave them peanuts and they went crazy, screeching and inviting all their friends to join the fun. Before we knew it we were surrounded with a whole troop of monkeys. Some other attractions in the park were the Impala observation point, Ivory burning site, Kingfisher picnic site, Hippo pools and the nature trails. By the end of the day we were exhausted. We conceived our first baby here in Nairobi - we were very excited! I tried to eat the Ugandan cuisine but was unsuccessful, feeling nauseated with pregnancy symptoms everyone could tell. I had a crash course in their mother tongue as most of the family in the country was not fluent in English. At the same time, we were getting troubling news about the political chaos in Uganda. I didn't know to what extent it was bad and had no idea of the civil war in Uganda until now. We had a lot of memories and reasons to remember Nairobi for a long, long time.

The Pearl of Africa

Uganda was called the Pearl of Africa due to its magnificent scenery, green landscape, wildlife and friendly natives (culture). The country was Africa's foremost safari destination in 1968. However, civil war in the 1970s and the 1980s destroyed the industry. The beautiful green valleys, vast lakes, tall mountains and mountain Gorillas where a spectacular sight that attracted a lot of tourists. By the time stability was restored in 1986, Africa's pearl was tarnished; big game had been heavily poached, hotel infrastructure was ruined, huge potholes on the streets and most of the buildings were destroyed. Kampala is the largest and evergreen capital city of Uganda. Initially this city was built on seven prominent hills, but now the city has spread over several hills and villages beyond Kampala's boundaries. At night, we used to see fire dancing on the hills from where we lived. Some said they were ghosts or witches and people were afraid to go up there. This beautiful place has a tropical wet and dry climate and seldom gets very hot during the year. Because of its high altitude the weather was cooler than other places on the equator. The city includes the Uganda Museum, Ugandan National Theatre, St. Balikuddembe Market (formerly Owino Market) and Nakasero Market where we did most of our shopping, mainly sweet potatoes as food was very costly and scarce at that time. In addition to Lake Victoria and the river Nile, Uganda is dotted with hundreds of other lakes.

A Man We Will Remember

Born in the country home in Igorora, the district of Ibanda in Western Uganda, Apollo Kataha was the youngest of fifteen: four siblings from his late aunt, (his mother's older sister who died) and three bothers and six sisters from his mother, who was his father's second wife. He was a Banyankole by tribe from the Ankole kingdom in Uganda and spoke Runyankole as his mother language. As a little boy, like all other children in the village, Apollo learned to work hard in school, on the farm and at home. The whole household was up very early to start their chores before going to school. The children fetched water from a far away stream, carrying big plastic cans on their head. From seven or eight years old, boys worked in and around the house as well as went to school. They accompanied the men to take cattle to the pasture and to herd cows, milk them, treat their ailments, and to protect them from wild animals, especially lions. Boys also learned to build and do manual jobs. Girls were taught household chores to prepare them for marriage. All the children learned to cultivate, sow, harvest, and guard crops against birds and animals. Children were also taught to bow and respect their elders and relatives. They had no electricity in the country and had to finish their school work before dark and be in bed before the oil lamps were put out. Apollo got his first footwear when he was 10 years old. He moved to Kampala to do his senior secondary school and lived with his brother in the city. Besides school, it was common for young people to clean, cook and take care of the house they lived in. He always scored exceptionally well in school and later on, won a scholarship by the Indian Government to finish his university in India.

Mother was fondly called 'Maaza' by the entire village. Apollo's mother was the sweetest to all, kind and very hospitable to everyone. He loved his mother very much. She and I got along very well with our broken dialogue and sign language. We laughed and sang spiritual songs together, she in Runyankole and me in English. She was a very godly woman and an elder in her Church. Mother died of old age around 92 years old. We had the privilege to visit Uganda again in 2006 and as the last and only living son Apollo performed the last rites at his mother's funeral. His father was an extremely strict man. He tailored colourful outfits and forced his kids to wear them to school, even if they didn't match their uniforms. A few months before our travel, he died of a heart attack. He collapsed while chasing cows up the hill early in the morning. All his brothers and sisters had big families of their own. They lived around the city and in their village home in Ibanda. The family had large herds of long-horned cattle as indicators of power and prestige. The district of Ibanda is a land of coffee, bananas, mangoes, passion fruits, pineapples, jack fruits and water melons. Almost everybody has banana plantations in the country.

Matoke (green steamed bananas) and millet is their staple food besides potatoes, cassava and maize (corn). Both men and women harvest, but the women winnow, grind, and thresh millet and other grain. Since the mid-1980s, AIDS has been a serious problem leaving many children orphaned in Uganda. They accept that old age is usually the cause for death and believe that God allows old people to die after the completion of their time on earth. The Banyankoles view death as a passage to another world. When a person dies, every relative, along with friends and neighbours are invited. Cows are slaughtered to feed all who are present and beer is a part of their mourning that goes on for four days. Witch doctors, voodoo, divination and witchcraft practices are common in most of Africa. But today, thankfully the majority of Banyankole and Ugandans are Christians.

The political crisis in Uganda was escalating when we arrived in October 1979. This once beautiful country from the moment you land at Entebbe's international airport, with its breathtaking equatorial location on the forested shore of island-strewn Lake Victoria was now unrecognizable. We were welcomed at Entebbe airport by Apollo's family - his oldest brother and wife and a few sisters. They hugged and greeted me, saying "Agandi Nyabo" which means "how are you madam?" I replied "Nimarung"' which meant "good." They called me Mzungu, a slang word for a white person. To them, I didn't look like the Indians living in Uganda. Most of the Asians in Africa came decades ago from Northern India, Goa, Gujarat, and Pakistan. I loved the colourful African outfits and the headwear they wore. They were excited to see their brother after years and chatted nonstop. Everything looked strangely different to me once we hit the road. This was not a dream. The forty-five minute drive from Entebbe to Kampala took hours. We were stopped at every check point by armed men in uniform. They searched us, questioned and examined everything. For the first time in my life I had ever seen a battalion of Tanzanian troops, Guerrilla soldiers and Policemen patrolling the streets, stopping cars and searching for what I could not understand at that time. It was hard to recognize who where the rebel forces and which ones were real. Driving through the capital city of Kampala the place looked deserted except for army troops and soldiers on the streets. After a long and tiring drive we finally reached our destination in the town of Mengo in Old Kampala.

The Ugandan dictator Idi Amin was overthrown by the Ugandan Tanzanian army and fled the country in April 1979, months before our arrival. A period of intense competition and fighting for power between different groups turned the whole nation into chaos. Northern Uganda had suffered from civil unrest since then and hundreds of people were killed in the rebellion against the Ugandan government, and an estimated 400-thousand people were left homeless. People risked their lives and ran into exile to the neighboring countries. Many hid; several expatriates and locals lived in hotels because families were attacked and killed in their own houses. Nights were silent except for the sound of shooting, people screaming and a smell of death. No one dared to move even in their houses at night for fear of being shot. Buildings were raided, shops and markets looted and people where robbed at gun point. The cost of food and essential items were sold in black market. There was constant fear and confusion. I didn't realize that this was only the beginning of a very long struggle that we would have to face for years to come, unless God by a miracle suddenly rescued us.

Not only was I in culture shock but this was the first time I had ever witnessed something so terrifying and dreadful. I was also pregnant with our first baby. More than anything, we had absolutely nothing prepared for our new baby and the shops here were totally bare. My whole world changed and I suddenly realized how helpless I was. All the excitement turned into fear and frustration all at once. We celebrated our first Christmas in the family house in Mengo, Old Kampala and by a miracle were able to find rice and meat for our Christmas meal. Each day was a miracle. I cannot even imagine mentioning all the dangers and challenges we faced every day besides the need for basic food and clean water. Months later I was introduced to an Indian family who came out of hiding after Idi Amin was overthrown. I believe God kept the whole family safe and alive just for us. Mr. George was the principal of a school in town and his wife was like a mother to me. They became my God-sent angels and helped me to prepare for my delivery. God supernaturally protected us and supernaturally provided for us more than words can tell. In one sense, we could never know how many times God actually protected us. However, in a world with free will to make our own choices, we can't get around the fact that hardships await us. But God has a perfect will for us and that includes different kinds of protection. I thank God not only for delivering us from what was happening but also for what could have happened but did not because of His 'swift grace.' I will always remember to thank my Lord for His constant provision and protection in our lives. We may not always know how the Holy Spirit protects us but we know for sure that He puts His angels in change over us. All I can say is; God is good all the time, and all the time God is good. Praise Him!

The Lord is my Shepherd; I shall not want.
He makes me to lie down in green pastures;
He leads me beside the still waters. He restores my soul;
He leads me in the paths of righteousness
For His name's sake.

Yea, though I walk through the valley of the shadow of death,
I will fear no evil; For You are with me;
Your rod and Your staff, they comfort me.

You prepare a table before me in the presence of my enemies;
You anoint my head with oil; My cup runs over.
Surely goodness and mercy shall follow me
All the days of my life;
And I will dwell in the house of the Lord Forever.

Psalm 23

Thank You Lord

Thank You Father for keeping us alive
When there was nothing else, nowhere to hide.
Shadows became reality, love You renewed,
Desires and dreams, You made come true.
When hate and fear was in the air
You held out Your hand and said I care.

Thank You for shelter away from home
You taught us to pray and trust You alone.
You changed our sadness into faith,
When all was lost, You told us to wait.
Exhausted and weary we could not fight
You said hold on child, trust Me through the night.

When people laughed and mocked in scorn
You nodded saying, it is Me they did wrong.
Death and dread tried to creep in our face
You turned them into escapes for Your names sake.
Angels You sent to make the way

To feed us and clothe us, our tears to wipe away.
You armed us with weapons to fight this war
Girded us with courage to say 'I am strong.'
Your heart may be heavy but not for long
My Spirit is with you child, whatever befalls.
Keep praying You said, You are winning the game
Milk and honey you will drink in My name.
Thank You Lord, You did it again!

Student Life, Marriage & Family

Chapter Four

Have you ever wondered about 'coincidences' that happen in an everyday life? There are so many outside elements that we have no control of in our lives, starting with birth, ending with death and including everything else in between those two events. Where you live, work, play or go to school; even where you shop, go to church and the people you meet, none of these are accidents; neither are they coincidences. There are no coincidences with God. Things just don't 'happen'. This is a superstitious belief. There is a divine purpose and reason for each and everything that happens in a life. That includes good and the bad things. He leads me in the paths of righteousness For His name's sake. Psalm 23:3. Although I was an unbeliever God already planned my life and was pursuing me. He gave me every opportunity to seek Him so I could find His peace even in the midst of trouble. Every new day creation itself declares the glory of the handiwork of God. Psalm 19:1. We are a chosen generation, a royal priesthood, a holy nation and His own special people. We are called to rise up for such a time as this. Peter 2:9. Predestined and preplanned before the foundation of the world. Ephesians 1:3-6. Our names are written in the Lamb's book of life. Luke 10:20. Until we come to the realization that God is in control, we try to help Him in our ignorance and works of the flesh. Once we know the great I AM, that He is above all things and He alone made all things out of nothing, then we can go out in confidence knowing that God has a reason for everything we experience in life.

Think about it, maybe you were running late, missed the bus and took your car or you were caught up in a traffic jam or suddenly changed direction at the last minute, only to find out later that you missed a major traffic accident that could've involved you. This literally happened the time I was writing this chapter. My son hesitated to take the bus that morning and drove his car to university only to find out later that the same bus had a major accident killing and injuring many people on the highway. What a miracle! Or you didn't have food to feed your family or milk for the kids and from nowhere someone shows up at your door with a bag of groceries. Better still, you had no money to pay the bills or funds for a mission project and suddenly you receive a cheque in the mail or someone paid for your airline ticket. These are called God Miracles! Such happen to people every day. They are the supernatural work and nature of God Himself. We too have experienced such divine miracles in many different ways! The deeper you plunge into this book, the stronger your faith will grow. You will believe that miracles are for today. God is doing extraordinary things in the lives of ordinary people. These adventures and real life stories exhibit glimpses of the Kingdom of Heaven on planet earth. As you read on, you will be encouraged, enlightened, and challenged to have a deeper walk with God and believe in Him as your Lord and Saviour. You may identify with our struggles and rejoice in our victories, while the real Hero who shines through these stories is Jesus Christ our Lord and Master over all. We believe miracles are for every day and they can happen to you!

The next few episodes of our lives are interesting but may be mind blowing for some. Definitely, they are not meant to seek attention to ourselves but dedicated only for the glory of God. Each story displays the power of God's love and His goodness in our lives. Not that we are fit (qualified and sufficient in ability) of ourselves to form personal judgments or to claim or count anything as coming from us, but our power and ability and sufficiency are from God. 2 Corinthians 3:5. Life is a precious gift and I am so thankful for every day. It may be hard to explain fairly how people, even children are forced to kill or be killed. All across the nation families experienced loss of lives, property and brutal attacks. Too many are not able to talk about them. Some have gone to their graves with heavy hearts. Others struggle to love and live, even now trying to cope with the heartaches of woe. At the same time young and the old have lost loved ones to malaria, HIV/AIDS epidemic and to other diseases. Millions of children have become orphans due to AIDS and countless women are widows today. Every family has a story to tell. My late husband Apollo was not able to narrate openly many of his personal experiences during those horrifying times. To give an account of the abuse of the evil and to seek out who is to blame is now useless. What good will that do, will it bring back what we lost? Who we lost? Yet, in all things I thank my Lord Jesus Christ Who by His goodness, abounding mercy and amazing grace supernaturally rescued us from Uganda's bloodiest bush wars, rebel attacks and some pretty mean people. Though we walked through the valley of the shadow of death and evil surrounded us, God's hand of protection kept us living. Death was on all sides, yet death had no power over me or my family. We are God's miracle stories living to face tomorrow because Jesus lives.

Memories of yesterday are still fresh in our hearts. Often we like to cover up painful situations or try to block unpleasant things from our minds, not wanting to talk about our fears and wounds. Silence may not be golden at all times; it can suffocate and even cause early death. When we speak up, our heavy burdens become light and even others receive healing. I could not question the Lord, neither was I able to understand why we were allowed to endure such dire hardships, but I know in all things God has a purpose. I am aware that countless communities and families need healing and closure from the past. For this reason, I am compelled to be a voice of comfort on behalf of millions of survivors, as well as my own children who were rescued as babies. They were too young to understand about food shortages and why they shared two cookies on a playground. That we travelled desperately back and forth from Uganda to India and back, like destitute, homeless wanderers. Sick with bronchitis, our two year old son would cry out for his mother and I was not there. Now in his thirties, he still carries scars in his heart that have turned to bitterness and hate for his parents. Our five year old girl still remembers hiding under the tables for fear, when the soldiers barged into her kindergarten school. Many others are screaming for answers. But our only answer is in Jesus Christ. He is our Comfort and Healer. He was sent to heal the brokenhearted... Luke 4:18-19. Our Lord came to this earth bottled in a human body, to walk in our shoes of pain, dying in our place so we can be forgiven, healed and set free. It is my honour to share in your pain and grief.

I Greta Kataha-Spica, wife, mother, grandmother as well as the widow of my late husband Apollo Kataha; a Woman of great faith, an Intercessor for family and the Saints and God's servant of the Gospel of Jesus Christ, take this opportunity to thank you for being heroes in the 1980s civil war in Uganda. We know that the scars, memories of crime and loss never go away, but together we can believe for restoration and freedom as we trust in our Saviour. There is power in the blood of Jesus to forgive and to heal us. Always remember, if one dream falls to the ground and breaks into a thousand pieces, never be afraid to pick up one of those tiny pieces and try again to love and serve others. Push forward and know there is light at the end of every tunnel. That light is Jesus!

If I didn't pass through those dry and dreary lands, I would not know how to lie down and rest in green pastures; to follow the Good Shepherd beside still waters and to sit at His banqueting table laid out in the presence of my enemies. Had I not experienced dread, emotional trauma, helplessness and hopelessness, I would not have love enough to forgive and to love others more. God taught me to walk in aggressive faith and to believe for the impossible. He wanted to reveal Himself as my Healer, Deliverer, Provider, Comforter, Shepherd and my Father. In humility together with Paul we too can say; I know how to get along with humble means, and I also know how to live in prosperity; in any and every circumstance I have learned the secret of being filled and going hungry, both of having abundance and suffering need. Philippians 4:12. When there was 'no one else and no way out' the Holy Spirit of power and might showed up. God's goodness and faithfulness never failed us. Every struggle shaped me to see something greater, far beyond the obstacles. They made me stronger and deeper in love with Jesus. Often God uses broken people to tell His love stories. We were broken in every way. We judge the vessel from the outside; by its looks, race, face, actions but the Lord judges His children from the inside; He knows the true intent of our hearts.

God's Divine Numbers

Amazingly, all our supernatural miracles and major events in our marriage and family happened in Sevens and in three phases of our lives. The first Seven years we had uphill battles running to and fro from war, fear and death. We endured many fiery trials together and we still survived. In the next phase the Lord supernaturally rescued my late husband Apollo and our two babies from Uganda's final and bloodiest bush war in 1986 and reunited us after three long years. We lived for the second Seven years in Manama Bahrain together as a family. The last and the third phase of our marriage was the best. We immigrated to Canada in 1995 and by November 4, 2000 we birthed a multicultural, non-denominational Church in the basement of our home in Mississauga Ontario. We served the Lord together for the last Seven years until the night before my husband went home to be with Jesus on December 4, 2007. All God's ways are perfect. His works are perfect and His Word is perfect.

Three and Seven are God's divine numbers! They are repeated through-out the Bible as symbols of completeness and perfection, both physical and spiritual. God's attributes are three; He is Omniscient, Omnipresent, and Omnipotent. The Trinity of the Godhead is three in One; The Father, The Son and The Holy Spirit. We ourselves are in three parts; spirit, soul and body. Peter denied knowing Jesus three times and later said he loved Him three times. Jesus prayed three times in the Garden of Gethsemane before His arrest. He was placed on the cross at the third hour of the day (9 a.m.) and died at the ninth hour (3 p.m.). Three is also the number of Resurrection. Christ was dead for three full days and three full nights. Jesus rose on the third day. God sits in the third heaven. 2 Corinthians 12:3. Time is divided in three past, present and future. The Number Seven is again God's number of perfection. From the Seven days of Gen-esis to the Seven Seals of Revelation, Scripture is saturated with the num-ber Seven. And on the seventh day God ended His work which He had done, and He rested on the seventh day from all His work which He had done. Then God blessed the seventh day and sanctified it, because in it He rested from all His work which God had created and made. Genesis 2:2. In the book of Revelation there are seven churches, seven angels to the seven churches, seven seals, seven trumpet plagues, seven thunders and the seven last plagues. The words of the LORD are pure words: as silver tried in a furnace of earth, purified seven times. Psalm 12:6. Jesus quoted seven parables in chapter thirteen of Matthew.

Synopsis of Dictator Idi Amin

Uganda was one of the lesser-known African countries until the Mili-tary Dictator Idi Amin came into power in the 1970s. His bizarre public announcements and weird advices fascinated the news media. Uganda was an African horror story identified with their former ruler, even a de-cade after. Amin was known as the 'Butcher of Uganda' for his brutality. During his presidency over millions of Ugandans lost their lives, in horri-fying ways. He had little education and joined the British army in 1946 as an assistant cook. Extremely charismatic and skilled, Amin quickly rose through the ranks. He was six feet, four inches tall and a Ugandan light-heavyweight boxing champion, as well as a swimmer. He soon became notorious among fellow soldiers for his overzealous and cruel military in-terrogations. He made the highest rank for a black African serving in the

British army and served in the British action against the Mau Mau revolt in Kenya. Amin mainly targeted the educated including 70,000-strong Asian community. He expelled the Asians in 1972, giving them 90 days to leave the country. In July 1976 he was personally involved in hijacking the French airliner to Entebbe. October 1978 Amin ordered an attack on Tanzania. He lived a lavish lifestyle contributing to the collapse of Uganda's economy. His rule was characterized by human rights abuses, political repression, ethnic persecution, extrajudicial killings, nepotism, corruption, and gross economic mismanagement. He gave his soldiers orders to "shoot on sight" anybody they suspected. Amin personally ordered executions of the Governor of the Bank of Uganda, the Anglican Archbishop, Chief Justice, Chancellor of Makerere University and several of his own parliamentary ministers. Several others fled into exile to Kenya and other neighbouring countries including some of our relatives. Tanzania invaded Uganda in April 1979; together with various anti-Amin forces they forced him to flee the country. He divorced five wives, had countless mistresses and married the sixth who was the mother to his last four children. He must have had at least thirty to forty official children. He died in Jeddah, Saudi Arabia on August 16, 2003. He was never tried for gross abuse of human rights.

History of Uganda Civil War

This once beautiful nation on the equator was rich in human and natural resources and great weather. From late 1970s Uganda struggled to end a period of political and economic chaos that destroyed the country's reputation as the 'pearl' of Africa. Meanwhile, the economy collapsed, infrastructure crumbled, wildlife was slaughtered by soldiers and the tourism industry evaporated. Thousands of Tanzanian soldiers who remained to assist with the country's reconstruction and to maintain law and order turned against the Ugandans. They took to the streets terrorizing civilians, randomly looting and killing people at gunpoint. Kampala suffered the aftershocks of too many bush wars. More and more school children were absorbed in the army and child soldiers were found everywhere, on road blocks and on the streets abusing the use of the gun. Homes were destroyed; communities dissolved and social life was paralyzed. Families hid in the bush to escape the atrocities of the northern soldiers. Many including a majority of Ugandan Asians left the country seeking asylum in other countries. Parents and children were separated. Malnutrition, starvation and disease escalated. January 1986 Yoweri Museveni became the President of Uganda and put an end to human rights abuses of earlier governments. He brought stability and economic growth to a country that has endured decades of rebel activity and civil war. President Museveni is currently both head of state and head of the government. Uganda has rebounded from the abyss of civil war and economic catastrophe to become a model of peace, stability and prosperity.

Angels Kept Us Alive

After the cruel dictator Idi Amin was overthrown, people including many Asians returned to Uganda. We arrived in Kampala during this most critical time. Our host family owned a transportation business and the brother was involved in politics. One evening while we were all together rebel soldiers raided the house. Mother-in-law had come from the country and the home was full of relatives and children. Armed soldiers pushed through the security guards at the gate, shouting in their tongue. Some of them opened fire on the streets while others ordered our husbands to follow them. Just as they left, we heard outbursts of screams, gunshots and confusion outside. We feared for their lives and thought they were killed. I had no clue what was happening and frightened they would return to attack us. Soon I realized that this was one of the many scary situations we would have to face in the months to come. Some of our maids ran away in fear and hid in the bushes. I was about seven months pregnant and they were concerned about me, especially Mother who was afraid I would go into premature labour. That night we stayed together in one bedroom, crying and praying. This was one of my first and worst experiences of dread and terror. I could hardly sleep, jumping up at the slightest sound wondering what was going to happen next.

In the African culture, people either don't know how or do not express their emotions in public. I have seen military personnel in India, living in army bases or in more peaceful settings but they never patrolled the streets with guns terrorizing, looting and killing people. So I was terrified! The next morning our husbands came home and we were so thankful they were alive. They didn't stay long nor say much but changed their clothes, picked up a briefcase and dashed out of the house as if someone was chasing them. They must have paid a lot of money to be set free. Bribery was the worst and number one corruption in Uganda in those days. I believe angels kept us all alive that day. The chilling dread of that

73

night never left us for a very long time. When day broke we prayed for night and in the night we prayed for day such was the agony of living in dread. My husband jumped up every now and then looking through the dark, frightened at even the slightest sound of a moving leaf. He couldn't sleep or rest. After more gun threats, my husband decided to leave and continue his masters in India. An aunt from the country came to stay until my delivery. Everyone around was talking only in their own tongue and I could barely get a proper conversation. Once in a while I played with the kids, took short walks and made friends with the neighbours. In my boredom I picked up a big fat book that stood out in the library and discovered it was a Bible. As a Roman Catholic I grew up knowing Bible stories but this was the first time I held a holy Bible in my hands. I was drawn to read it from cover to cover. When I got a chance to go shopping, I searched for baby products and towel nappies (diapers were unavailable then) in almost bare shops, collecting two nappies here, three there and a few items of baby toiletries. So I started hand sowing small outfits from my own cotton wear. A Christian family I met some time earlier suddenly showed up in my life again and helped me prepare for my delivery. The birthing stories of my children during these times of chaos and curfews are special miracles that I will narrate in a separate chapter.

Weeks after my delivery, I accompanied the family for a political campaign in the country. It was a long eight hour drive, on bumpy, red muddy roads. I remember the first time I came to Ibanda with my husband. The whole village showed up. Over a hundred folks gathered in the family house to greet us with music, drums and singing. His Mother, all the elders of the clan, his siblings and their families crowded this place. As their tradition, they presented us with a goat and a special drink made from fermented millet. I was introduced to this huge family and made small talk with Mother and the sisters. We walked up and down the hills enjoying the country side. This was our baby girl's first visit to her father's village. The house was on a hilltop surrounded with farms, fruits trees and the scenery was simply breathtaking. I loved the country and their special tea made with fresh cow's milk. Now this place was packed with campaign supporters, relatives and neighbours. They slaughtered cows and feasted the whole day. It was good to see a lot of familiar faces of family and friends again.

First Journey to India

 By a miracle when we got back from the country I was given airline tickets for us to travel to India. It was exciting to show off my new baby girl to her father and my family in India for the very first time. Things did not go well in India. My mother had no room for us. No one was willing to listen or care to understand our plight in Uganda. This was no surprise because we had no money, didn't carry gifts and people already despised our marriage. They were expecting the worst for us anyway. We were helpless. We visited relatives in Erode, our old railway town and they ignored my husband and made him feel very uncomfortable. He was the only black African in that whole town. They kept their kids away from our baby girl and behaved very strangely. Belinda at four months looked different from the other children; she was gorgeous, fair skinned, sharp eyed doll with a cute Afro. Yet I couldn't understand the mindset of a racist even among my own people. I found nothing wrong with race or colour. The African people are lovely; or any people for that matter. I am a people person who enjoys multicultural diversity, different foods, styles and the richness of every culture is beautiful! We came back to Bangalore and sold all we had including my jewelry, got a hotel room and made plans to leave. We survived on five Indian rupees a day, eating apples for breakfast, lunch and dinner. On our flight back to Africa the baby got sick with vomiting and diarrhea. Thankfully we had a stopover in Bombay (Mumbai) and rushed her to a clinic. We proceeded on our journey, heading back to Uganda to face our fears and fate once again.

We Had Dreams, God Had Plans

 There are no food stamps, food banks and second hand clothing stores in Africa or in India at that time, like they do in North America. In the third world, life can get pretty difficult especially for a mixed race 'black' couple. During the long period of guerrilla, bush wars, we traveled in and out of the country searching for safety, fighting against all odds to raise our young family. Although we had a bad start we believed this was only for a short time. Prior to my marriage, I worked all through college supporting my mother and younger siblings until I left India. I had cleared all my mother's debts from a large sum of money I won in a court case. Before leaving India the first time, I visited a dying aunt in Mumbai to recommend my sister to get her inheritance. All our wedding expenses, travel, etc., were taken care of by me. I owed no man a thing except love. No matter what people did to me, God gave me a special fondness from a child to forget and to innocently love more. This is not to blow my own horn but to show you how quickly the good is forgotten and now I was a laughingstock. When everyone else shook their heads in disappointment over our helpless situation, we knew in our hearts that God had a bigger plan. We were isolated, ridiculed and rejected on every side. Relatives in Muscat Oman refused to reply to any of my urgent pleas for help. In Uganda families owned businesses, plantations, farms, fields in the country and yet when a supply of food was brought into the city we were deliberately left out or given scraps. To people we looked pathetic and defeated but in God's eyes we were more than conquerors ready for takeoff. Romans 8:37. When your back is against the wall and there is nowhere to run, look up. Let His face shine on you as you learn to bask and rest in Jesus The Son. If all hell breaks loose stand your ground and watch you soar from defeat to victory. These are the painful lessons we learned along the way. God is sovereign in all His ways and never overlooks the desperate. When we receive His love we can love others unconditionally.

Back in Kampala, we rented a one bedroom suite in the heart of the city. People could not live in houses for fear of being attacked by rebel groups. Things had gone from bad to worse; the streets were messy with deep pot-holes due to the bombings and neglect. Most buildings and houses were broken down and by now everyone was learning to cope with the after effects of war and high inflation. Every day was bad news. In the night we heard shootings and people crying and running in terror. Randomly people were missing or put into prison. Women lost their husbands and children to the cruelty of war, starvation and disease. More fighting broke out to overthrow the new Obote government. Guerrilla groups and rebel armies emerged to sabotage the new regime. By this time many of our family and friends were gunned down and lost most of their possessions. We were happy if we found a loaf of bread for two hundred shillings. A five pound bag of sweet potatoes was fifty to seventy shillings and we tried to have one meal a day. Soon the currency was changed and they were carrying a briefcase of paper for the same value that lasted only for a week. Each passing day was a miracle even if we had no food. Once we were so dry for days that I was forced to borrow a cup of baking flour from a couple of women in the hotel to cook a meal. My husband was desperately looking for work. He had relatives in influential places but they refused to help him.

Sitting on the twelfth floor balcony of Apollo International Hotel, in the heart of the city of Kampala with our baby girl, we used to pray and together dream big about our future. We desired to work in the Middle East, travel the western world and to do big things with our lives. My husband promised to buy me a car. We imagined driving to work and going shopping instead of walking up and down the hilly, mud roads sweating in the scorching heat. He desired to replace all the jewelry we sold and to buy us new clothes. We planned for more children and that they would have the best education and live blessed lives. At this time we had no clue when and how anything was going to change. In actuality we had absolutely nothing. All we had was prayers, words and carried away in our daydreams. It looked simply impossible. Down the road, the Lord began to restore us in every area of our lives. Our prayers were being answered one by one. Supernaturally, suddenly and swiftly our dreams, desires, longing of the heart and every thought came into reality just as the Bible promised. We were mightily blessed to be a blessing to others and especially to all who offended us. We became everyone's favourite as we ministered to all who came our way, including relatives from both sides of our family. These God stories only exhibit the bigness of our great big Lord whose faithfulness reaches to the heavens. Every heart needs to hear the sound of heaven so you too can move mountains and let God turn your situations upside down and inside out to bless you to be a blessing. What a faithful God we serve!

Our Badges of Honour

We may reflect on these incidents from time to time with a sigh of relief wondering how we made it 'through' while others did not. Neighbours and friends suffered many violent attacks and were brutally killed. We were confronted and intimidated by rebel soldiers who took all we had yet in each and every situation our lives were spared. Due to malnutrition and multiple malaria attacks I suffered excessive bleeding and a miscarriage. I was still breastfeeding my one year old baby girl. When I went for a checkup, the doctors carried out a procedure I could not understand. I was confused - was it a miscarriage or an abortion? People did anything to rip money off you in those days. Health care was costly and primitive; it could have taken my life with their lack of equipment and medicine. Everyone else thought nothing of it but I was suffering the loss of my unborn baby. My body was failing me. Deep down there was a vacuum.

'No one understands the mysterious sorrow of losing a child that never actually was allowed to live.' Not even my husband knew what to do or say. Our baby Gabriel is now in heaven waiting to cheer us in through heaven's pearly gates. Some of these hidden scars tell our secret stories that have now become badges of honour for God's glory.

Curfew in Kampala was from 6:30 p.m. to 6:30 a.m. and anyone found on the streets during this time of the night was in danger. Even shadows through your window can entice rebels or thieves to break in. I was pregnant with our third baby and going for regular checkups in Mengo hospital. It was common to be stopped by armed soldiers at check points. They either demanded money or anything they could demand for just to let us pass. This time it was different. They stopped us and took my husband away, leaving me and my little girl alone in the taxi. At a distance, behind the thick bushes I heard gun fire and loud voices. I began to panic and pray. Half an hour later my husband returns robbed of his watch and money but they spared his life. He watched people being shot and was forced to kill others, which they normally do. He didn't speak of that incident ever again. Jesus warned us that; the thief does not come except to steal, and to kill, and to destroy…. John 10:10. A demonic spirit of death was all over the town, but miraculously we walked under a cloud of divine protection. After the birth of our son we were attacked by rebel soldiers again and forced out of our home.

Journey to India with the kids

My husband worked for the Uganda Chamber of Commerce and was selected for Sussex England on a special project for two years. After we lost our home at gunpoint, we lived here and there with relatives. While he was going to be away in the UK, we decided I take the children to India for a while. As usual, soon the home front was tense. Now my Mother couldn't handle the kids running around in her small house. She got us out of the house. This time I was in a worse situation. I had two coloured children less than three years old, no money and desperately helpless. Everyone was feeling sorry for us. Someone took me to a convent in Bangalore to leave the babies for adoption. When we went to sign the documents of consent the next day, I suddenly realized that I would never see them again and I immediately cancelled the adoption. I thank God from saving me from making such a foolish mistake I would have regretted all my life. My sister was a single mother with two kids so we rented a house together and helped each other take care of our children. I worked, took care of the kids and waited for my husband's return. The children celebrated their birthdays and began to fret for their father. It was time to travel back to Africa. In the meantime, I ran into an old friend on vacation from the Middle East who promised to help me find work in Dubai. We agreed this was the best solution that will help us leave Uganda once and for all.

The children were happy to see their father again and I was excited to share the good news with him. We had hopes and a silver lining was beginning to show after all. Gladly my husband agreed to take care of the children while I worked in Dubai. We waited for my visa and began to make preparations for my new adventure. This separation was not going to be easy but we had no other choice. I was so broken with the thought of leaving my family and especially the kids who were barely two and four years old. Before my travel, we stayed up most of the night crying and praying. I woke up early. I know our parting was going to be very difficult. We trusted each other and we trusted in God.

My Supernatural Escape

When I arrived in Dubai International Airport, my friend and the Arab sponsor came to meet me. At the airport my documents and passport were taken away. I was going to work for this man's travel agency the next day. This was my first journey to the Middle East and I was unaware of the Arab culture. I trusted my friend who I knew for years. Here I was a young married woman in my late twenties, away from my husband and little children and didn't know what I was getting myself into until the next day. Soon enough I realized that I was cheated and was amongst sick, Arab Muslim perverts. When it comes to women, Arab Muslims are dogs not only to their own women but to expatriates as well. My mind was on the job; how I could rescue my family and when I would get to see my babies again. A few expatriates from other Asian countries also worked for this travel office. I felt something was not right; he had cameras in all corners of the building and his employees were edgy. By evening when everyone left, my friend didn't come to pick me up. I was alone with this weirdo. He pulled down his office shutters, directed me to a room and put on a video. I was new to Dubai, didn't know my whereabouts and I was tempted to give in. But although I needed the job so desperately, I became angry when he touched me. As if an angel was directing me I suddenly observed a side door and walked out on the streets. The Arab came running after me trying to pull me aside. With all the bad experiences I suffered earlier in life, I learned too well how to fight such men who acted stupid. I got wild, raised my voice and started hitting him. He didn't want to make a scene so he agreed to take me to my friend. My escape was nothing but a supernatural miracle of God. Some folks who work in the Middle East, expatriate men and especially women will do anything to keep a job or to earn extra money. Through the years I have witnessed many young girls caught up in such sex trafficking rings, exploited and mistreated. I was almost going to get myself into a lot of trouble but GOD in His mercy and grace sent His angels to snatch me out just in time. I have no words how to thank my Jesus for saving me in that hour. The next day, the Arab was furious and he was going to deport me. I was an Indian passport holder so I demanded for an air ticket to India knowing too well how difficult it would be to leave Uganda again. I was utterly disappointed and worried yet in my heart I was still hoping.

Seven Supernatural Favours

I was miserable and desperate living without my children in Bangalore. Only a few months ago I was here with them but now I was so alone. Weeks turned into months and I was frantically searching for another job anywhere in the Middle East. My relatives tried to discourage me as usual. Then I met this friend who introduced me to an agent selling work visas for a small Island in the Middle East. He was hiring maids for a Sheikh's palace in the Kingdom of Bahrain. Not having the huge sum of money he asked for, I desperately agreed to exchange my body for the visa. I was actually prepared to sell myself and take a risk to try and save my husband and children from the ongoing civil war, the starvation and the threats of death hanging over their heads. That is how desperately troubled and worried I was. I was like an insane woman ready to do anything at this stage. This was my only chance to get out and take the biggest risk of my life, at any cost. In a few months I got the visa for Bahrain and was on my mystery journey. I swore, that this was going to be the last time India would ever see me poor and helpless again.

On arrival in Bahrain airport, I was met by the agent who again took my documents. I was taken to a house with a group of housemaids from a few different countries. None of them knew English well. Some were from India and Sri Lanka. Soon I found out that one of them was pregnant by her Arab sponsor and was sending her back home. She was confused, ashamed and was attempting suicide. Even though I had no idea what I was doing here, or I believe everything happened for a reason. The maids in that house were to be sold as sex slaves, including myself. A woman in desperation will do anything to save her family. Those women were in similar situations like me but in a different way. They slept on the floor and I was given a bed. *Favour number one.* At night I heard some being raped but no one dared to come near me. *Favour number two.* I lay in bed praying to escape or ready to fight. God supernaturally hid me and sent His angels again to protect me. The next day one of the girls took me to the Catholic Church in Manama. *Favour number three*. I met with the priests and asked for prayer for my desperate situation. Later that night when everyone was asleep, I quietly sneaked out of the house and ran in the dark straight to the Catholic Church, hoping I would find someone. To my surprise, Vincent De Paul Society members where having a party and they welcomed me in. *Favour number four.* I stayed with people from the Church that night. *Favour number five*. After a few days the Society and the Catholic Priests organized a meeting with the agent and my Arab sponsor on my behalf. *Favour number six*. By a miracle the Arab Sheikh immediately signed my release. *Favour number seven.* God's love is amazing! Even in our foolishness and sinful ways, He is ready to forgive us and love us more. I am forever grateful and cannot stop praising my Lord and King.

While I waited to find another sponsor in Bahrain, I helped in the Church and worked with a Priest doing his wooden art work. People were very generous to me. In the meantime I got news that another war broke out in Kampala and all communication was cut off. Everyone was praying for the safety of my family. During those times of desperation and uncertainty my favourite song was, 'one day at a time sweet Jesus.' That song kept me strong and gave me hopes that my Lord would carry me through from day to day. Times like this mean people always show up to add to your pain. One prominent person in the Church took advantage of my plight and brought me to her house to wash dishes. Another woman in the Society had me babysit her grandchildren who were the same age as my babies. It broke my heart thinking of my own children without proper food and care. An American Priest came to see me at the house one day and was so moved to hear about my family. He promised to help me and said, 'Greta I will pray and find your family in Uganda whatever it takes.' At the same time I got a job as a Secretary (today's administrative assistants) for Ashraf Brothers, one of Bahrain's oldest and most prestigious retailers and wholesale distributors on the Island. I found favour with the management because of my skills and soon I was promoted to an Accounts Assistant. I was able to rent my own 'one room apartment,' bought my first eighteen inch TV set and a mini fridge. Praise God from whom all blessings flow. Heaven's plan was beginning to unfold in our lives.

Father John, like a God-sent angel and I called Uganda almost every day until we found my husband in his office and planned their escape. Glory to God! They were all safe, alive and eager to finally leave Uganda. The Church and the Society helped me raise funds for my family to leave the country and to travel to India. I was able to provide for their stay anywhere, as long as the Lord made it possible for us to be reunited. After almost a year, my German boss, Mrs. Ashraf helped me get visas for my husband and the children to enter the Middle East. Like a dream come true, God made the impossible possible. They came on a two weeks visit visa and stayed in Bahrain for the next seven years! What a mighty God we serve!

Psalm 91 Protection

Because of the turmoil in Kampala, people were sacrificing their lunch time and having prayer meetings everywhere. On September 1985, my husband was speedily running home after shooting broke out downtown when a friend invited him for an afternoon prayer fellowship. In that meeting he received Jesus Christ as his personal Saviour and instantly the Holy Spirit filled him with a new life of joy, peace and hope. Jesus washed his sins away and adopted him to His royal priesthood, Holy Nation and made a unique person out of him. Amazingly from a little boy of five he knew God had chosen him and given him a desire to love and seek His righteousness and forgiveness. Many times he asked God to 'forgive him and to protect him' but he didn't know that was prayer. After he received Christ, in the midst of fiery battles he found peace. Immediately he knew there was a calling in his life.

Three months later, again the bloodiest civil war broke out in his Kampala. Terror, despair and a spirit of death raged through the city. Soldiers were breaking in, looting and killing people leaving heaps of corpses on the streets. When they came to their area my husband was afraid and surrendered the whole family to God. Although he won an award in school for memorizing the Bible, now he could only remember Psalms 91. He hid with the children and his sister's family in a small bathroom for three days, under foam mattresses. All their windows were shattered. After three days of heavy gunfire the battalion of soldiers left. A sudden silence fell upon the town and he peeked out to look for a way to run and get food. The sky was thick with smoke, dead bodies lay everywhere and every building was broken into. The soldiers attacked the entire neighbourhood except this house. The soldiers came near their house but did not touch this door; it was an amazing miracle! Except for being shaken in fear of the loud bombardment and being without food, they were all safe. God sent His angels and supernaturally protected him and the children that day. You shall not be afraid of the terror by night, nor of the arrow that flies by day. Psalm 91:5. My husband ran over dead bodies to see if his brothers were alive and to search for food. Early 1986 the civil war in Uganda ended. The Lord kept my family safe and alive to fulfill His purpose in our lives in the days to come.

I pray you will be challenged with our real life stores to move into deeper depths and higher heights in Christ Jesus. We must continually reach for greater truths to go on in our Kingdom walk, willing to be pioneers of faith yet daring to tread in realms of the Spirit that are unknown to the natural man. There are no limits in God. We must break down the limitations that have been imposed upon us by the mind of man and boldly believe for the fullness of the Spirit in our lives. To know Jesus Christ in a greater way, to bear His image of love and to know our place in His Body should be our longing desire. This is the burden of my heart and God's heart for His children as Jesus prayed, Father make them one as You and I are One. John 17:20-22. The revelations you will receive from this book are not the ultimate of God. But as you and I eat off His Word and grasp the Truth, the Holy Spirit will draw back the Veil and reveal more of the glory and beauty of Jesus Christ. If you are of His fold, you will hear and recognize His voice through these pages, and you will know that you are being introduced to deeper truths. You too can walk in intimacy with Jesus the anointed One.

The Father Heart of God

The love of the Father is so awesome. I know that my Jesus loved me before I was every born, when I had yet no days. Your eyes saw my substance, being yet unformed and in Your book they all were written, the days fashioned for me, when as yet there were none of them. Psalm 139:16. Before I called out His name He answered me. He preserved me, hiding me from wicked men and the enemy of death. When I was abandoned and alone He never left me once. Love will cause you to forgive seventy times seven and even more every day so you can freely live in the Father's love. The secret and only key to receiving His blessings is in forgiveness! Let God do your fighting. When the enemy comes like a flood, the Spirit of the Lord will raise a standard against him! Isaiah 59:19. We may fail a hundred times, but we can still get up, dust off and begin to trust God to do even greater and bigger things if we glory in His presence. He is waiting to show off Himself in and through you. We are created for our Father's pleasure just as we take joy in our own children; let the Lord sing over you with great joy. Get ready for takeoff and let the Spirit of the living God take you to higher ground!

Great and marvelous are Your works,
Lord God Almighty!
Just and true are Your ways,
O King of the saints!
Who shall not fear You,
O Lord, and glorify Your name?

For You alone are holy.
For all nations shall come and worship before You,
For Your judgments have been manifested.

Revelation 3:15

One Day at a Time

(A Song that kept me alive throughout my desperation)

I'm only human, I'm just a woman
Help me believe in what I could be and all that I am
Show me the stairway I have to climb
Lord for my sake, help me to take
One day at a time.

One day at a time sweet Jesus
That's all I'm asking of You
Just give me the strength to do every day what I have to do
Yesterday's gone sweet Jesus
And tomorrow may never be mine
Lord, help me today, show me the way
One day at a time.

Do you remember when You walked among men
Well Jesus You know, if You're looking below, it's worse now than then
Pushing and shoving and crowding my mind
So for my sake, teach me to take
One day at a time.

Chorus

Reach For The Stars

When your back is against the wall and there is nowhere to run,
look up if all hell breaks loose,
stand your ground and see
To every blessing from above,
forgiveness is the key.
You will soar on eagle's wings and reach for the stars.

Let His face shine on you as you turn to the Son
Climb every mountain before your time here is done
No matter what others may see, do or think
Your life here is planned,
your destiny won't blink.

Before time began,
before you were even born
You were fashioned for greatness,
to dream beyond your call
The Sun of Righteousness shall arise with healing in His wings
And you shall go out and grow fat, like calves in a stall.

India 1980

From Uganda to India 1986

India, 1983

Bahrain 1987

Chapter Five

The miraculous continued to follow us where ever the Lord led us individually and as a family. I know you are stirred up with curiosity for more of the supernatural. Signs and wonders of the Lord are poured out only by the grace of a loving heavenly Father. The unearned favour of God challenged us to seek after Jesus and to grow from faith to great faith, to demonstrate and witness the most difficult, unheard wonders only the Holy Spirit could make possible. The Bible says without faith it is impossible to please God. Hebrews 11:6. The righteous will live by faith. Romans 1:17. Faith sees the invisible, believes the incredible and receives the impossible. To have faith is to have confidence in the One Sovereign Lord who is able to do anything but fail. If there is no faith there would be no living in this world. Fear is the opposite of faith and it is from the enemy who is a lying thief and a murderer from the beginning. Jesus gave each one a measure of faith as small as a mustard seed. We must have faith and trust in God who never changes. He does not lie nor does He slumber or sleep. When heaven comes to earth, the supernatural has no choice, but to come along with it. This is why miracles followed Jesus wherever He went. The first miracle Jesus performed at Cana of Galilee was for the purpose of manifesting the glory and nature of God. He only does what He sees His Father do. This miraculous entrance stirs an appetite for the supernatural miraculous God. Jesus brought heaven to earth and heaven is naturally supernatural. We honour and obey God by sharing what He has done in our lives so we can bring life and salvation to a dying world. Faith is the bird that sings when dawn is still dark. Another way to have powerful faith is to associate with others who have great faith.

Desperate Hope leads to Daring Risks

There is something called desperate hope, but nevertheless it is hope. Risk results in rare, weird and life saving miracles. God's grace is sufficient for the day to carry us all the way. "One day at a time sweet Jesus" became my song of the day. Finally we were able to leave the terror and dread in Uganda behind us and move on with our lives. There was no going back, at least not for a very long time. My family arrived in Bombay (Mumbai) India and house by Christian friends. They went shopping, sightseeing and relaxed for a few days before taking a train down south to Bangalore. My job provided for all their needs. The children started school in Chennai. Every day we wrote letters and sent greeting cards to each other. I was able to send gift parcels and money orders every month and we waited for our next move. Those who do not understand desperate hope live at ease in king's palaces. They do not understand the hardness of life. People who are not oppressed by illness, sorrow, afflictions and troubles, do not understand how a drowning woman can clutch on to a straw in desperation. One who has never suffered need will not know how to appreciate water, food and even a peaceful night's sleep. When I heard them mocking, I would tell myself that the Maker saw their mockery and saw my need. Desperate to be reunited as a family, I tried every means to rescue them. My husband Apollo suffered humiliation by most of his relatives especially after he was left alone with the kids. When I made plans to rescue my family, they thought it was a joke. But now that I started working in the Middle East and the family was rescued from Uganda we had great hope. Freely we could communicate and together we believed that one day we would be rewarded for holding on. I hoped even when I had no hope left. I know the Lord had a special place in His heart for the sorrowful. His eyes were on us just as His eyes are on the ant and the little sparrow.

Thank God, my desperate hope and deadly risks saved our lives! When one is cornered in all directions, no one hears the cries of a relentless heart like Jehovah God, our Omnipotent Father. He was my Father even when I didn't know Him. The different names of God only represent His many attributes. To every need I had God revealed Himself as my Jehovah God the Lord over every situation. Another word for Jehovah is Adonai, the Lord of lords. He is Yahweh the Eternal Living One. That men may know That thou, whose name alone is Jehovah, Art The Most High over all the earth. Psalms 83:18. Jehovah Rapha, the Lord who heals – Exodus 15:26, Psalm 103:3. Jehovah Jireh, the Lord my Provider - Genesis 22:14. Jehovah Nissi, the Lord my Banner – Exodus 17:15. Jehovah Shalom, the Lord our Peace – Judges 6:24. Trust ye in the LORD for ever: for in the Lord Jehovah is everlasting strength. – Isaiah 26:4. This is Jesus; the most high God over all gods. His loving kindness is better than life. He made all things beautiful in His time and now everyone was able to see our victory.

A friend invited me to a "Jesus Calls Crusade." After work a group of us drove down to the Indian school in Isa town for the meeting. This was a prayer ministry founded by the late Evangelist DGS Dinakaran from South India. As a depressed young man, the late Brother Dinakaran was unable to bear the anguish of poverty, sickness, unemployment and failure and was walking towards the railway tracks to end his life. On the way he was met by an uncle who told him about Jesus. He came home and prayed committing his life to the Savior and God filled him with the Holy Spirit and joy. In an encounter with Jesus during family prayer one day, he received Christ's heart of compassion to pray for other hurting people. Now his son, Paul Dinakaran has expanded this prayer ministry across the world. Unfamiliar with such Gospel meetings at first, I was disappointed the Evangelist didn't call out my name and give me a word of knowledge as they said he would do. I was restless that night and took time off work the following day to meet him and ask for prayer. I waited in a long line and he finally prayed with me and said, "Daughter, you will weep tears of joy, your family will soon join you." With this joy and boldness I headed to meet my German boss to request for visit visas for my family. Amazingly, without any hesitation she approved and helped me bring my husband and the children to Bahrain within ten days. Just as he prophesied, I became ecstatic with joy!

Bahrain, in the Middle East

Kingdom of Bahrain is a small island country situated near the western shores of the Persian Gulf. The name 'Bahrain' is from the Arabic word Bah, meaning 'sea.' Saudi Arabia to the west is connected to Bahrain by the King Fahd Causeway. Iran is to the north across the Persian Gulf and the peninsula of Qatar is to the southeast. The capital city of Manama is home to many large financial structures. Bahrain participated in the Second World War on the Allied side. On August 1971 the State of Bahrain declared independence. It became a Kingdom in 2002. Summers are extremely hot in the Gulf. The seas around Bahrain are very shallow, heating up quickly and producing high humidity, especially at night. The weather may be up to 50°C (122 F). Rainfall is minimal and irregular. Arab women suffer discrimination and for a long time were not allowed to participate in public life. Their first female MP was elected in 2006 and by 2011 there were four women in the parliament. In 2008 they appointed the first woman ambassador to the United States making her the first Jewish ambassador of any Arab country. Since 2005, Bahrain annually hosts a festival in March, titled Spring of Culture. Bahraini people are ethnically diverse. The state religion is Islam. Non-Muslim Bahraini citizens are mostly Christians. Expatriate Christians make up the majority of Christians Community in this small Island.

Our Miraculous Reunion

The family arrived Bahrain mid June of 1987. This was actually happening! No man could perform such a miracle but my God! He brings dreams, desires and the longings of the heart into reality. No matter how long it takes, if you don't give up your eyes will behold the glory of God. It was worth the long, hard wait. Finally my long lonely days and nights would soon be over. In my small one room apartment, I had pictures of my family all over the place. My dresser was full of dolls, cars, trucks and stuffed toys of all sizes waiting for my daughter and son to arrive. We were not going to lack or starve ever again. No one knows hunger pangs unless you've been through it. Bahrain is a land of full and plenty of every kind of fresh food readily available. My Christian colleague took me to the airport. That was one of the biggest and best days of my entire life. When you're helplessly waiting for a miracle to happen and finally it is here, how does one contain such joy? Days of fear of the unknown and begging for crumbs are no more. Now, there is nothing left to do but shout and weep for joy. My Lord was bringing my miracles to me. The Bible says; weeping maybe for the night but joy comes in the morning. Psalm 30:5. I couldn't eat or sleep just thanking the Lord for His great faithfulness. He was making it possible for me to actually see my husband and two babies after almost three long, painful years.

They walked through that airport lounge and my heart wanted to scream for joy. We hugged with excitement and swore never to part again. My daughter Belinda was soon going to be seven. She held my hand as if never to let me go. Roy was five and by now he'd forgotten me and calling me 'aunty'. We walked hand in hand with indescribable joy as if the whole world belonged to us. My one room apartment was like heaven to us, it was filled with everything we needed. It didn't matter how tiny it was as long as we were together. A real tiny bath and kitchen and the space could only hold one double bed, a small TV on top of my mini refrigerator and a make shift couch. We cherished our freedom as a family and held on to each other never wanting to let go. The following month of July was a celebrating of three birthdays. Belinda turned seven and we were both thirty two years young. No words could express our gratitude and joy. At this stage we didn't have a car so we walked everywhere; to Church, shopping center, Bab Al Bahrain Souq and took long walks to the Marina beach.

What we think is important at times can quickly change to what really are priorities, like family and loved ones. You will realize that if you ever have to choose between time and money again you would always choose time. Time to be with family, your spouse, children and with those you love. The reason we share testimonies, is to invigorate and excite us so we keep remembering that God is alive and at work in our midst. Bless the Lord, O my soul, and forget not all his benefits. Psalms 103:2. We simply honour and obey the Lord by bearing witness to His love. Psalm 22:22. Sharing binds the church together as we open our lives to one another rather than keeping a distance. Listeners are stirred up to praise God and to reflect on their own lives. They are encouraged to believe and receive their own miracles too. We overcome the enemy when we share. And they overcame him by the blood of the Lamb and by the word of their testimony. Revelation 12:11. Those who fail to testify often lose the blessings they previously received. It does not mean that we will never be tempted or fall again. Jesus, who is the perfect Son of God, was tempted. Not that we will never fail again but it is simply confessing what God has done according to His promises. It is thanksgiving, praise, and giving glory to God. By sharing, we also pass our faith on to our children from generation to generation. Deuteronomy 6:7. Most importantly it gives worship to God. The one leper who stopped to worship and thanked Jesus is remembered to this day. Luke 17:16-19. Let us not be like the other nine but instead look for opportunities to glorify God and to be a blessing. Another way to teach the Word is by sharing your real, miracle life stories.

Holy Spirit Encounter

The Lord had done many great things in our lives, yet I was still giving glory to my dumb idols, rosaries, infant Jesus and novenas. I heard about Jesus but I did not know Christ as my Lord and Saviour. My husband tried to explain the miraculous wonders they had experienced and how they escaped many dangers. At that time I had no idea of the supernatural working of the Holy Spirit. The nail pierced hands of Jesus did miraculously protect us from time to time. Either I was not aware or had not given much thought about the saving grace of God. A few friends and relatives were "born again believers," but I always ridiculed them. Because of my upbringing as a staunch Catholic, I was confined to man's word rather than believing in God's Word, the Bible. To the religious, Jesus is some distant, pathetic figure still hanging on a cross. We give importance to Mary, the Saints, and angels rather than to Jesus the risen Saviour. He suffered, died and forever lives to lead us to the Father through His Holy Spirit. I had a cute altar everywhere I went; with lifeless idols and radiant statues decorated with flowers. We were going to the Catholic Church and prayed the rosary every night. My husband was a very patient and loving man, he read his Bible every day. I was too proud to notice any change in him, because I thought I knew it all. We moved into a two bedroom apartment and gradually the blessings of the Lord were overtaking us.

We sat down for family prayer as usual on night and I was troubled in my spirit. Quietly in my heart I asked the Lord to show me how real His Word in the Bible was. I wanted to know if my husband was right in believing God differently than me. Something was happening to me that night. I sensed a heavy garment over me but could not understand it at first. Feeling like a heavy log of wood I just could not move. The next day it was the same weighty presence, like an embrace and a peace came over my whole being. I could not open my mouth to pray. The third day, I realized it must be God, I felt a sweet presence again come over me and I froze. I tried to open my mouth to pray and suddenly I began to blabber something funny. Strange words were coming out of my mouth. It felt like a river was pouring out of me and I got louder and louder. I did not want to stop. I was baptized in the Holy Spirit and began to speak in a heavenly tongue. I can still remember the time, the place and that night so clearly just like it was yesterday. God was doing something so supernatural in my life and I have never been the same ever since. Today, Jesus is physically appearing, visiting many religious people with God encounters all over the world. Time is running out and He's rounding up His sheep who will hear His voice in these last days. It is not about religion by whatever name or method is used to reach the only Creator, Maker of heaven and earth and everything in between but it is about a love relationship with Jesus Christ Himself who will do anything to bring His children back to the Father's house. Why he offered to die in our place on the cross. Religion controls us with rules and traditions of man. But there is freedom in Christ. The Anointed One came to earth to build His Kingdom as He prayed; Thy will be done on earth as it is in heaven. Jesus is our bridegroom and we are His bride. He is the Good Shepherd and we are His sheep.

Everyone and everything else had come and gone but Jesus came into my heart to stay forever. He has never left me once nor will He ever. I didn't say any sinner prayers like most people do. All God was looking for was my heart, my hunger to know Him. My husband taught me the Bible and explained my experience with the Holy Spirit from the Book of Acts. Praise the Lord! Right there I heard the Lord say to me, "you have Me in your heart, now you don't need those idols." I was radically changed. That very night the altar and the idols came down. I was 'born again' into a brand new creature from the inside out. Everything looked the same on the outside but something new had happened on my inside. My heart was on fire eager to pray and to know the Holy Spirit more. Like a light switch went on, the blinders came off and suddenly my spiritual eyes were opened. All the past, pain, weaknesses, struggles and heartaches vanished in the blink of an eye. Until now I had received nothing free from anyone. But now without any rituals, chanting, beads, idols, hidden agendas and no obligation to man, I was completely set free. Jesus paid my debt I could not pay and He washed all my sins away. The wickedness of my sins was so great and too many but God's mercy and grace saved me and washed my slate clean. For the Scripture says, "Whoever believes on Him will not be put to shame." Romans 10:9-11. The Holy Spirit filled me to overflowing and gave me the Gift of Eternal Life absolutely free. Hallelujah!

Baptized in the Holy Spirit and being filled with the Holy Spirit are one and the same experience. Acts 1:5, 2:4. The Holy Spirit can infuse churches with boldness and equip them to impact communities and lives for Jesus Christ. When the Holy Spirit Fire ignites your dead sleeping spirit, the light comes on and suddenly all sin, darkness, generational wickedness and curses are broken. John the Baptized said; HE will baptize you with the Holy Spirit and FIRE. His winnowing fan is in His hand, and He will thoroughly clean out His threshing floor, and gather His wheat into the barn; but He will burn up the chaff with unquenchable fire. Matthew 3:11-12. Only then we are led by the Holy Spirit of power and might. Until then, man is blind leading the spiritually blind. Today, we need the Holy Spirit more than ever.

- To be witnesses. The disciples were baptized with the Holy Spirit. Acts 2:4.
- To edify oneself. Speaking in tongues edifies. 1 Corinthians 14:4.
- Boldness to speak the Word of God like Peter. Acts 4:31.
- Power to heal with signs and wonders. Acts 8:12-17
- Fulfill the threefold command: Repent, Baptized & Receive the Holy Spirit. Acts 2:38
- Radical transformation. Saul became Paul. Acts 8:3; 9:1-2.
- Overthrow prejudice. Acts 19:6
- Spiritual gifts to flow in the Body of Christ. John 1:32-34.
- Church is strengthened with the gifts of the Spirit. 1 Corinthians 14:26.

To our surprise my husband soon got a job with the Marina Club and started work the next day. He entered the country on a visit visa and needed a work permit to work in the country. He found favour with God and with man and a miracle happened. Mrs. Ashraf's daughter was in charge of the immigration department where I worked. When she got the news about his job, she was furious and sent us to the Criminal Investigation Department, police station. The officer in charge was very angry and wanted to imprison us until he could deport us back to Uganda. An officer was writing down our report and something happened. The Holy Spirit walked in that room and changed everything in an instant. Glory to God; mighty to save, heal and deliver us from every evil plot of the enemy! Suddenly the angry shouting officer calmed down and came where we were. My husband jumped up and handed him his bosses' contact information. He stopped and took the piece of paper and walked away. After a long discussion with the Marina Club Manager, the CID officer returned to apologize to us and said we were free. The two men happened to be friends. Amazingly, our immigration problems were solved right there and then. If you are familiar with the immigration process in the Middle East you will know it is costly, tedious, and a lengthy process to get work permits and family visas in the Gulf. But God did it again! Neither of the men knew about our family situation at that time and on the phone our entire family's residence permits were sanctioned at no cost. Only a great big God is able to make the impossible possible over and over again in our lives, so the world can see Jesus lifted up through us. We were excited and consumed with the Spirit of God that we walked out of that police station laughing with joy. God's love knows no limits, no boundaries. He fought every battle for us like He always did. We are totally dedicated and surrendered to Jesus, the Author and Finisher of our faith. We will always remember to give Him all the glory, honour and praise for the great and mighty things He had done for us.

Mystery of Love and Intimacy

There is no love as awesome as the love of our heavenly Father. A love that is greater than all love. Every mother has a fraction of this kind of love to a certain extent; from the time of conception, before she sees her child she loves that baby unconditionally. No matter the colour, hair, eyes, toes or any defects, a mother loves and prepares for her blessing with joy. This is great love, but God's love is even greater. We have not yet scratched the surface of the abounding love of Yahweh God. His love melts our hearts to forgive, suffer and die for one another. We are created like our heavenly Father, in His image of love, made in love and we have the capability to love. The Holy Spirit helps us to love in such a manner. If we as imperfect beings can love our children unconditionally, how much more the Creator and Author of love can love us? Jesus loves you more than you know. Do not be afraid to receive His love today. Unless you grasp this secret, man is busy chasing the wind, running to and fro, trying to work out love in the flesh. God's desire is to overwhelm you to overflowing. As you soak in the tangible presence of God, you will begin to know that you are truly and totally loved, maybe for the first time in your life. Soaking may seem a crazy word in intimacy. When you soak and meditate on the Word of God, you are able to hear His whispers, His soft voice that is able to change you from glory to glory. As high as the heavens above so great is the measure of our Father's love. Even when we fall away, His love finds us and draws us back. Love never gives up. Love always wins! Love will teach you patience, endurance and to rest even through stress, pain and struggles. Intimacy with Jesus is to abide in this love. that Christ may dwell in your hearts through faith; that you, being rooted and grounded in love, may be able to comprehend with all the saints what is the width and length and depth and height - to know the love of Christ which passes knowledge; that you may be filled with all the fullness of God. Ephesians 3:18-19. The shed blood of Jesus and His amazing grace forgives us and makes us free to forgive and to love others unconditionally. We can love, pray and care for others just as Jesus the perfect Lover of all lovers loves us.

Our battle to live together as a family cost me my job with Ashrafs. God knew I badly needed this break. I was suffering with painful, crippling arthritis which became worse with time. A pastor and his wife came to visit us and brought an audio cassette of Richard Roberts from the USA, 'Is Healing for Today.' As I was listening to this message, I was led to break hereditary curses, abnormal birth (I was born a blue baby) and to forgive any and everyone who hurt me. At the end of the message I prayed with Richard and received my healing. I felt a burning sensation over my hands and feet and I was healed from arthritis that day. Weeks later our son Roy was healed of bronchitis. Some great things were happening to us in this small Muslim Island. We attended the Catholic Charismatic meetings during the week and joined a full Gospel fellowship on Friday evenings. Weekends in the Middle East are on Thursdays and Fridays. I struggled to leave the Catholic Church until we were warned in a dream of an incident that actually took place. Confusion arose between the Priests and the Charismatic leaders who refused to say the 'hail Mary' and many left the Church.

We were planning for our reunion baby to celebrate the goodness and faithfulness of God in our lives. This was perfect timing. I was off work and the two older children were in school. I got pregnant for the third time. The following year our son was born. I was offered a job with the U.S. Foreign Buildings Office in Zinj when the baby was two months old. My husband bought me my first car, a beige Toyota as he promised on the hotel balcony in Kampala. We were now a two car household and our dreams were kicking in. the blessings of the Lord gave us amazing favour and great joy.

One morning my boss was crying in his office because his mother in the U.S. had a ruptured appendix and was in emergency surgery. I prayed with him and the next day he reported that she was out of danger and recovering in care. That opened a door to share my testimony and to pray with him on several other occasions. At the end of my contract, I got a job with the U.S. Embassy on an entry level. I was one of few Christians among the staff and soon everyone knew it. Some attacked me for my faith but some knew where to come for prayer when they had a need. A colleague was suffering with abnormal bleeding after her third baby and we prayed in the photocopy room. She received the Lord and a while later came back to testify that the bleeding had completely stopped. In two years I was promoted to a Secretary in the same department. Months later I was offered a promotion in Administration to work for the First Secretary of State, third in line from the U.S. Ambassador. Once again the Lord raised me up to one of the highest expatriate positions in the U.S. Embassy in Bahrain. I was chosen to receive foreign diplomats and VIP guests for their July 4th, Independence celebrations. Among other duties, I processed Gulf visas for U.S. Staff, Diplomats and military personnel especially during the Iraq Kuwait, Gulf war crisis

U.S. Operation Desert Storm

We survived another war in Bahrain, the first Gulf War from August 1990 to February 1991. This was a conflict between Iraq and a coalition force from thirty four nations led by the United States and mandated by the United Nations in order to liberate Kuwait from Saddam Hussein, the political leader of Iraq. Bahrain was the primary coalition naval base and the point of origin for coalition air operations against Iraqi targets. Bahraini pilots joined other members of the coalition in flying strikes into Iraq. The war is also known under other names, such as the Persian Gulf War, First Gulf War or Iraq War. Operation Desert Shield was the U.S. operational name for the U.S. buildup of forces. We were advised to store water, food and other emergency supplies during this time and hid at the sound of every siren. The Embassy distributed gas masks and safety outfits to all their citizens and staff. The Island is very small; it could take just one scud missile to destroy the whole Island but three Scud missiles were aimed at Bahrain and by a miracle two were directed into the sea and one on land but did not hit any target. All the Churches and Christians on the Island were in prayer 24/7. We believe the Lord sent His angels to protect the Island and kept us safe. February 27, 1991 President Bush ordered a cease-fire. Operation Desert Storm ended the ground campaign in 100 hours of ground combat. Iraqi soldiers, demoralized by the air campaign surrendered in masses. After the Gulf war everyone working at the embassy received a 'Certificate of Appreciation' from Operation Desert Shield/Storm.

August of 1990 for the very first time, we took a vacation to South India as a whole family. We were now blessed with three children. The Lord was prospering us and making everything new in our lives. I was reluctant to see my folks again, but the Lord directed us to carry the Gospel to my household. We were reunited with all my siblings and their families. Each one of them was having issues with health, marriage and in their own lives. Our on time God planned our travel just for them. People were in awe to see and hear the wonders the Lord had done for my family. Listening to our miracle stories many folks were beginning to come to the Lord. Three days before we left India, my whole household received Jesus. My mother was 65 years young when she prayed with us one night and was radically changed when the Holy Spirit touched her. An older brother was healed from tuberculosis and the holes in his lungs miraculously closed up. A relative's marriage was restored and after a long wait her husband got a job in the Middle East. God was doing amazing miracles all around us just as we prayed. Believe on the Lord Jesus Christ, and you will be saved, you and your household. Acts 16:31. The Word of God was fulfilled before our eyes. Salvation is an individual action. They were not saved because of us or anything we did. But they were saved because they believed the Gospel message of the Bible and responded in faith to the invitation of the Holy Spirit. Jesus said; No one can come to Me unless the Father who sent Me draws him; and I will raise him up at the last day. John 6:44. This is the sovereign love of the Father; He is continuously drawing His children into the fold. When we hear His voice let us respond to His call today for yesterday has gone and who knows what tomorrow will bring.

The Full Gospel Church of Philadelphia became our spiritual home. The main Praise and Worship Service was early on Fridays at seven in the morning, followed with fellowship and Bible study in the Church Villa. Friday night worship was in Awali, a thirty minute drive across the Sitra Bridge. This was one of the first English speaking, registered full Gospel Churches on the Island. We had cell groups throughout the week in various Asian languages. Now each cell group has become a Church and together they are one big multicultural Church in Manama. God started using us together and separately in Bahrain. After my husband's graduation from Bible College he was ordained to preach and lead worship serves. I started women's groups in one nurse's hostel and soon was holding Bible study and prayer meetings in three nurse's hostels. Men and women come to work in the Middle East from all over the world particularly from the Asian countries. Most expatriates live alone without their families and desperately need fellowship, prayer and are ready to receive the Gospel. Today many of those Saints have carried the saving message of Jesus Christ to their towns and nations and like us some have started their own ministry. We opened our home for cells groups, deliverance ministry and intercessory prayers meetings during the week. My husband and I supported each other's ministry and served the Lord together within the Church and community. We also duplicated and circulated Christian audio and videos of teachings, music and ministry tapes to any and every-one who was open to receive the Gospel message including local Arabs.

Hearing the Voice of God

It is important to recognize God's voice. He speaks through His Word, His people and through the gifts of the Spirit, 1 Corinthians 12:2-3. We may also receive messages of warning and exaltation in dreams and visions, Numbers 12:6-8. Creation itself declares the glory of God. Psalm 19:2. I know beyond the shadow of a doubt that God still speaks today. To hear God's voice we must belong to Him. Jesus said, My sheep listen to My voice; I know them, and they follow Me. John 10:27. Those who hear God's voice belong to Him; they have been saved by His grace through faith in the Lord Jesus. These sheep spend time in His Word, abiding in Christ and they recognize Him as their Shepherd. He who dwells in the secret place of the Most High Shall abide under the shadow of the Almighty. Psalms 91:1. The secret place is in God's presence, spending time in Bible study and meditating on His Word. The more you talk to Jesus, the closer you will draw to Him and YES, soon you will learn how to 'Recognize His Voice'. While God could speak audibly to people today, He speaks primarily through His written Word. Most of the time a tiny voice within our own conscience lets us know when we are not on the right path, prompting us to stop and think before we proceed. The Lord always speaks to us in that 'still, small voice.' 1 Kings 19:12. Like the voice of many waters, and like the voice of loud thunder... Revelation 1:15 and 14:2. If there's no peace in what you hear or receive, it's not from God. The Holy Spirit is not the author of confusion so let His peace and joy rest on you as you seek Him today.

Our Journey Continues

After the Gulf crisis, people were paying a lot of money to immigrate to Canada. We too put in an application for Ontario, paid a minimal fee and waited on the Lord. We failed the interview held in the UK due to discrimination but we enjoyed a short holiday in London England. In the meantime the Lord started speaking to us through visions and prophesies. Once, we attended a house meeting where no one knew us. The Spirit of the Lord revealed that we would soon be leaving the country and He was preparing a place for us. This was confirmed by a visiting preacher in one of our Church services. In another prayer meeting, the Lord showed someone in the group a map where we would be traveling to and she said a letter was in the mail to confirm our departure. At this time no one was aware of our plans to leave the Middle East even though we were seeking the Lord for direction. We believed if God opened a door no one could shut it. To our surprise, months later we received a letter from the Canadian Consulate in Riyadh, Saudi Arabia about our immigration process to Canada. We thought our case was closed in the UK and we forgot all about it. We had no idea how Saudi Arabia had got our files but we believed God was at work and we were excited. The best part of the letter was they were coming to Bahrain to interview our family.

By this time we had one daughter and two sons and I was pregnant with our fourth baby. We asked the Lord for a second baby girl and He gave us the name 'Rachel.' We held on to that promise. Many joked about the sex of the baby and were amused that even without having an ultra sound, by faith I was certain it was a girl. The Canadian interviewers came to Manama and finalized our immigration process to Canada at no extra charge. We gave them the name of our baby girl and waited to send them her birth certificate. What a mighty and faithful God we serve; He never stops surprising us with His amazing love. Our beautiful baby girl was born just as our hearts desired. Months before our departure we resigned from our jobs. In prayer one night, the Lord gave me the exact date of our travel to Canada and confirmed the same to my husband in his shower. May twenty third 1995, our family of six traveled to Ontario to start our new lives. Before our journey, the Senior Pastor, Deacons and Elders of the Full Gospel Church of Philadelphia ordained us as Evangelists and released us to the nations. The healing and deliverance ministry followed us to Ontario Canada. Our move to Canada was a fulfillment of the Lord's promises in 1989 and the calling to serve Him for the rest of our lives. The price of victory is high but so are the rewards. Victory at all costs, victory in spirit of all terror, victory however long and hard the road may be; for without victory there is no survival. Heat of the battle is as sweet as the victory. Only in the Word of God do we have faith to win and receive everything the Lord has already won for us, if we only believe! Your victory is right around the corner, never give up.

But God, who is rich in mercy,
because of His great love with which He loved us,
even when we were dead in trespasses,
made us alive together with Christ (by grace you have been saved),
and raised us up together, and made us sit together
in the heavenly places in Christ Jesus,
that in the ages to come He might show
the exceeding riches of His grace in His kindness
toward us in Christ Jesus.
For by grace you have been saved through faith,
And that not of yourselves;
it is the gift of God, not of works,
lest anyone should boast.

For we are His workmanship,
created in Christ Jesus for good works,
which God prepared beforehand
that we should walk in them.

Ephesians 2:4-10

At Heaven's Pearly Gates

When you go home in the blink of an eye
Will you look out and feel satisfied?
When your race here is run and life's journey is done
You sowed seeds of love and thought you had won?
Will they be family or friends to surround,
To bear your witness and show you around?

Should I go before you, I will wait.
Standing and waving at Heaven's Pearly Gates.
With Saints and loved ones we will cheer,
Looking out, excited as you draw near.
Worshiping Jesus Christ our King and Lord
Singing and dancing in one accord.

Come to that place, the mansions' so great,
You won't be disappointed, don't miss your date.
With the angels and a cloud of witnesses we will stand,
The beheaded and babies who left this land.
Friend this place is real, forever true;
Jesus' blood saved me and you.
Beloved, we will meet at Heaven's Pearly Gates!

July 4th, U.S. Embassy

Sitra Bridge, Bahrain

Before Leaving To Canada

Ashrafs Christmas

Gulf War Masks

Chapter Six

Human beings are created as sexual beings, male and female, so we might have intimate relationship with each other as husband and wife. Genesis 1:23-25. God created us out of His love in His own spiritual image. He conferred with Himself; The Father, The Son and The Holy Spirit and said, Let us make man in our image, in our likeness, and let them rule over the fish of the sea and the birds of the air, over the livestock, over all the earth, and over all the creatures that move along the ground. Genesis 1:26. The family is a masterpiece of God's Creation. Then He said in Genesis 2:18. It is not good that the man should be alone; I will make him a help meet for him. Therefore, the family was not man's idea but God's design, plan and pleasure to reflect His love on planet earth right from the beginning. Marriage and parenthood reveal His character. Children are added blessing and an extension of the family designed by God. They experience love and learn how to love others in a family. Listen, my son, to your father's instruction and do not forsake your mother's teaching. Proverbs 1:8. In marriage we bear offspring and join God in the procreation of other human beings. Three of the Ten Commandments are of the family. Commandment five, Children are to honor their father and mother. Seven, thou shall not commit adultery. Commandment ten, thou shall not covet thy neighbor's wife. One of the marks of Christian maturity and qualifications for leadership is the quality of the Christian home and family. An elder must be blameless, the husband of but one wife, a man whose children believe and are not open to the charge of being wild and disobedient. Titus 1:5-6. How amazing it would be when husbands and wives are faithful to each other in marriage and children honor their parents to live a long and prosperous and everything goes well with them! Less crime, no wounded people and no room for broken lives.

Fight for Your Marriage

Interracial marriages, mixed black marriages were not common in India. I may have been one of the few in the whole nation to marry a black African. We prayed, worked hard and fought to keep our marriage alive. Our relationship was based on love. Even though my husband Apollo and I were from two different worlds, race and culture we had similar values and life goals and we laughed at the same things. We wanted adult lives that were different and better than our parents. In days gone by, people frowned at interracial marriages. Some communities even banned marriages between whites and blacks. They began to define and label all interracial relationships even longstanding, deeply committed ones as illicit sex rather than marriage, that it was contrary to God's will and somehow 'unnatural.' Today, all mixed marriages are common and accepted. Don't be fooled: the enemy wants your marriage; he wants any marriage to fail. He is a vicious opponent without mercy. If you won't fight for your marriage, he will. Bless God, we paid a price by enduring many obstacles and fighting to keep our love and marriage last till death parted us as husband and wife.

The difference between a 'Relationship and Religion' is like the difference between a Love marriage and an arranged marriage (set up or forced). One is purely out of Love for Jesus and the other out of force, to please ancestors, parents and man. One takes no effort just obedience, trust and surrender to our holy eternal Bridegroom Jesus Christ and the other has a list of 'dos and don'ts' to please matchmakers, go-betweens and traditions of man. One is free as a Royal, the other in bondage as a slave. If you trust God, He can still turn your 'arranged marriage' into an exciting, intimate Love Relationship. Whom the SON sets free is free indeed! John 8:36. A customary practice of an arranged 'cast' marriage is worse than an interracial marriage. It's terribly wrong to live the rest of your life with someone you don't love just to please parents, for the purpose of bearing fair children and being a maid to your husband and in-laws. People have been doing it for years and many women suffer discrimination and abuse. Hopefully this has declined through the years.

The very fall of man put husbands and wives at odds with each other. Marriage in general is not easy, it takes hard work. Any two people living together will have issues if we cannot accommodate and love each other unconditionally. This is only easy when the love of God rules our hearts, marriage and homes. He can rescue every marriage if there are two willing people to make it happen. Whatever condition your marriage may be today, you need to fight for it. Work on intimacy in your marriage. Trust and believe in your spouse. Prayer is simply said, hardly done. Pray for your marriage and your mate. Eliminate distractions: media, internet, throw out edgy movies, and accept purity in your marriage. Marriage is like a triangle; Jesus is the head and the center of it all. As you and your spouse draw closer to God, you will draw closer to each other. Forgive quickly, some things seem unforgivable but we must pursue peace at any cost and obey God. We will have conflicts but communication goes a long way. We didn't start that way, but through the years after a lot of screaming, crying and pouting the Holy Spirit caused us to calm down and 'have cool heads' as my dear mother would say. That doesn't mean you have to live in an abusive, dangerous or unfaithful marriage. Let your husband lead your home; submit to him and agree to disagree when necessary. If you doubt him, pray that God will speak to his heart. If you have an unbelieving husband, practice I Corinthians 7. Our marriage was not perfect, it may never be, but it is real, good and it will last. The only way to a moral reformation is a spiritual awakening, and the only way to a spiritual awakening is the preaching of the gospel. The only people who can preach the gospel are those who experience true love with our Lord Jesus Christ. Let your marriage reflect the love of Christ. 'Sorry' and 'Thank you' help along the way. My new husband Fred fights for me and my emotional health by taking me out on dates, looking for my favourite ice-creams and getting me out of the house. We've grown in ways we didn't know were needed and still working at it. The process of becoming one is never ending, and when both work at it, the effort leads to deeper intimacy and stronger love.

Conceived in Nairobi

Of all the joys and challenges in life, nothing is more extraordinary than having your first baby. My husband Apollo and I conceived our baby in the city of Nairobi on our stopover in Kenya. Right from the womb this child became my best friend and only companion most of the time. From pregnancy to birth, a woman experiences so many changes. That amazing glow to those precious first baby kicks, there's so much to love about expecting a first baby. Of course, any mama-to-be will tell you, there are also those pregnancy symptoms that are far from fabulous. I had it all, the morning sickness, nausea and the smell of any food made me sick. We were head over heels in love with our baby and started picking names for a boy or a girl. When we got to Kampala, the family didn't know we were pregnant. Then one sunny afternoon, while chatting with my brother-in-law out on the lawn, suddenly I fell in a bang in front of them. I fainted and my husband lifted me like Tarzan and carried me into the house. They immediately went searching for food. No matter the circumstances and challenges we faced, I absolutely enjoyed all my pregnancies. They were a part of me, my body was carrying a living soul and that alone excited me. All my children had normal healthy births and were beautiful. The older two were born in Mengo hospital in Kampala and the younger son and daughter were born in Salmaniya hospital in the Kingdom of Bahrain. The best part of a marriage is when a couple bears forth a new person that resembles themselves. God commanded man to be fruitful and multiply. Genesis 1:27-28. Women are created not only as helpmates to their husbands but also for birthing both in the natural and spiritual. I was learning new things every day. A mother's love is like a circle, it has no beginning and no end. The unconditional love between a mother and child is amazing; it grows with excitement each passing year even as they grow into adults. There are two wonderful gifts I heard them say we can give our children - Root of Love and Wings to fly. Each one of my miracle babies has an interesting birthing story of their own.

With the growing insecurity and inflation in Kampala, I learned new ways to cope with myself and the baby. The shops were looted, bare and cost of living and baby items were unimaginable. I sowed baby outfits from my own cotton clothes and found a few towel nappies here and there. (Diapers were not available then). We were threatened and robbed at most security check points. That was Kampala in those days. When I was seven months pregnant the entire family suffered a rebel attack and I was badly shaken. That day the Lord miraculously rescued our husbands from being gunned down and supernaturally protected the rest of us. Weeks before my delivery, like 'God sent angels,' a Christian family blessed me in ways I will never forget. I badly needed the break to get strong and they helped me prepare for my baby.

For a first time young mother it's difficult to know when you are in real labour. Like most new moms I made a few trips to the hospital. I was worried about Kampala's healthcare and their primitive medicals conditions. Yet in the midst of all the chaos and mess, I anticipated a miracle. An off

110

duty nurse friend (like an angel), stayed with me till the baby arrived. On the third night they were preparing me for a 'C' section. After the tests, shaving my stomach, my brother-in-law signed the papers of consent and we waited for the doctor. I was on a liquid diet, drinking dry tea the whole night. I heard women screaming during child birth and I was afraid. One mother was having her eighth baby and they were beating her to push in order to save her baby's life. Robina and I prayed for a normal delivery. She tried to delay the surgery until the morning. By midnight the contractions became stronger and more frequent. After hard work of pushing, the baby was finally born and normal. July seventeenth 1980, around 2:30 Thursday morning our princess daughter was born. I hemorrhaged badly. They also gave me a tear and after the delivery stitched me without any anesthesia. Again I grabbed on to my friend's arm digging into her skin gritting my teeth in excruciating pain. But suddenly everything changed in an instant. Nothing can describe a mother's love and joy when she first sets eyes on her baby. All the tiredness, pain and fear are replaced with untold excitement, fulfillment and peace. Giving birth is one of the most intense, exhausting, amazing experiences in a woman's life. I had no idea that pain to such an extent was a natural part of labour. But I know every woman is unique in the level of pain they can tolerate and God miraculously helped me through. I was so proud of myself.

This was the day I was waiting for as a first time mother! Nine months of excitement and preparation. Belinda was the most beautiful baby in the world, simply perfect! She was light skinned with a small afro and flat nose. People laughed at my pot belly when I was pregnant making rude remarks about a 'tar ball baby' but now nothing mattered. I kept thanking God for my birthday gift. She came just one day before my twenty fifth birthday. At home, I was on a continuous supply of milk chai (tea) and maize porridge. They tried to bath the baby in a basin of steaming herbs and she screamed, I screamed and that never happened again. The families in Uganda were Protestants and organized a feast to baptize the baby before I left to India. Her god-father gave her a new African name 'Kamshuka' to add to Belinda. She was about four months old when I traveled to India. Her father was thrilled to see his little baby girl; she resembled him in so many ways. Every head turned to look at our pretty doll face princess and complimented us with smiles.

Belinda was twenty two months when her baby brother was born. She'd climb and sneak into his crib to carry him. One day I caught her lifting the baby, his head hanging and she was kissing him. I didn't have a camera to capture that picture but she was a very caring sister to all her younger siblings and that sight was beautiful. I learned to tie her on my back Africans style to keep her from mischief or to put her to sleep. Women in Africa work in the fields and walk distances with their babies on their backs. My husband was going to the UK on a work assignment for a year and due to the instability in Uganda I was forced to take the children to India for a while. This child missed her father and cried all through the flight. No sooner had we arrived in Bangalore, she put her little finger in her Nana's fan. She fretted for her dad, was a fussy eater and after some months she was hospitalized with jaundice. The morning before I left to Dubai, this four year old woke up very early to help me pack and make pancakes. She still makes good pancakes! As little as she was, she tried to comfort me. We embraced, made our promises to each other, kissed and said goodbye. She remembers armed soldiers coming to her kindergarten class during the war in Kampala. The children hid under tables and their teacher tried to protect them. She was a typical African sister to her little brother comforting him with hugs and kisses especially when I was not there. When the family escaped to India in 1986, Belinda used to send me letters with drawings and we exchanged red lipstick kisses even on the envelopes (this became a family trademark). We reunited in Bahrain in 1987 and celebrated her seventh birthday with a big 'B' cake. She turned fourteen in Canada and celebrated every other birthday every since. She always giggles and says; I am International; conceived in Nairobi, born in Uganda, lived in India, raised in Bahrain and now a Canadian!'

A father's love is so unique, it cannot be replaced. Her dad had a special place in his heart for his little girl and gave in to her fancies even as a young adult. She loved spending time with him polishing the cars, watching him build the deck or just to sit and talk. He took her for her first hair perm and taught her to ride her first bicycle in Bahrain and gave her driving lessons in Canada. Like most mothers, I taught her to become a walking, talking, singing doll and took her first baby steps with her. The first time she fell and bruised her knee I too cried and made a big fuss over it. We started the mother-daughter dates in her teens. I think this is important so children can comfortably share their fears, concerns, and discuss sensitive issues. As parents we thought we were doing well but later realized that we failed to understand the peer pressure and teen issues she was facing in school. Thankfully with much prayer and the goodness of God she turned out bolder and stronger. We celebrated Belinda's eighteenth birthday party with a big bang and lots of her friends in the basement of our house which became her private castle until she got married and left home. An email I recently received from Belinda, quotes; "Hi Ma, do you remember when we finally reunited in Bahrain and I was almost seven? You came to pick us up from the airport and brought a Vintage shut eye doll. Then when we got home to that one room apartment I saw over twenty more dolls of different shapes and sizes. I don't think I ever said thank you enough. Thanks ma! I was so happy seeing you and that doll. I still remember that moment. Shout out to my Preacher Parents for raising me right. Exotic and intelligent! Love You, Belle." End quote. I agree a girl's best friend is her mother.

At our daughter's wedding, both her father and I walked her down the aisle. He then had the honour of officiating the ceremony and pronounced them husband and wife at the end. Their first and best father daughter dance was beautiful! She got her first car as a wedding gift. On our twenty eighth Wedding anniversary Belinda organized a date for her father and me in the revolving restaurant in Niagara Falls Ontario. All the trials and hardships we have faced as a family, taught her also to be a princess warrior and to stand up for others. Married to Sheldon Barrocks a great husband who supports her dreams, Belinda is now a mother of four beautiful children herself. A motivational speaker, mentor to young girls and women, an award winning entrepreneur, she also won the best Black Canadian Photographer award two years in a row; for 2014 and 2015. The Lord bless and keep my daughter Belinda and her household in His plan to show off His glory through her life, family and business. May she continue to mount up on eagle's wings, conqueror every obstacle, be a world changer and impact lives for the Kingdom of God. Isaiah 40:31. This song was composed and dedicated to Belinda to strengthen her faith and walk in the Lord.

No Fear in Me

When I am with Jesus, there's no fear in me
When I am with Jesus, I know He'll care for me.

I know that He loves me, He even died for me
He's building my mansion
And He'll come and take me home.

I know that He blesses me, He is so pleased with me
He promised to use me, until the end of time.

When I am with Jesus, there's no fear in me
When I am with Jesus, I know He'll care for me.

Miracle Baby, Our First Born Son

After the loss of our baby Gabriel in a miscarriage, I was depressed and no one to talk to. In my day, pregnancy is not something one planned for, it just happened. When one is married it is but natural to have children and raise a family. Couple of months after our loss, I was pregnant again. We took no precautions and no pregnancy tests. All the symptoms, lack of menstruation, breast changes, morning sickness and fatigue was proof enough. There were no prenatal, birthing or breastfeeding classes and no internet for free lessons in the 1980s. We played by ear, instinct and reason. Nevertheless, there was a certain charm in the way pregnancy was diagnosed in those times. Today we can clinically pinpoint ovulation and conception. An ultrasound can determine the sex of the baby and you can take pictures in the womb. It wasn't too long ago that women couldn't get an official diagnosis until mid-pregnancy and the moving of the baby in the fifth month. There is an excitement and joyful surprise after a baby is born that cannot match anything. We were both young, wanting to grow with our children and ready for our second baby. Financially we were unprepared for any of our children but God always had a good plan. I knew this pregnancy was not going to be an easy one. My body was already weak from the miscarriage; breast feeding and we barely had food. This baby was going to be extra special, to help overcome our loss. I took long walks every day pushing my girl in a stroller up and down the streets, telling stories and singing songs. The situation in Uganda was getting worse with anti-government guerrilla attacks causing insecurity and rebels on the street threatening human life. Anyone found after curfew hours was attacked and shot. Even shadows through your window can entice rebels or thieves to break in. People were forced to leave their homes. We moved several times for fear until we found an apartment. Soon we would be a foursome family and that was exciting.

This time we were hoping for a boy. Although our oldest was a girl, the first born son is always special. He carries the family name and passes it down the line. My late husband Apollo always said; a son adds to the family while a daughter subtracts. A girl will get married and come under the husbandry and leadership of her husband's family. A son's place is always in his father's family. The first born son has two meanings. The first is more literal, the fact that this son is the first son born to his father; a man's strength, pride and joy. The second meaning refers to the rights and authority of a person, because they are the firstborn; he stands as a priest to the Lord's service on behalf of his family.

Sunday evening we took an early walk, I was feeling discomfort and a mild backache. It was steady and gradually increasing. We ate our Ugandan meal of kalo (ground millet) with meat stew and started packing my hospital bag. This was my husband's first experience with labour, (he was in India for my first daughter) he wanted me to try and hold on till the morning. As the contractions progressed, he got frantic and tiptoed in the dark to get neighbours to help. One old woman came with a blade in case of any emergency. He finally got hold of a phone and called the hospital but they refused to send the ambulance. The police too were afraid to come for fear of guerrilla attacks. After continuous phone calls back and forth, around four in the morning a police jeep pulled up in front of our house. My husband stayed back with our daughter and my neighbour friend accompanied me to the hospital. The streets were bare and scary, thankfully we got there safe. Deep potholes and broken roads on the way made the ride bumpy and dangerous. I could have delivered in the vehicle clinging on to my friend and a policeman in fear and pain during each contraction.

We reached the hospital just in time. I was rushed straight to the labour room. The baby was ready and I was in the final stages of labour. Again the Lord sent an (angel) nurse who without delay popped the water bag herself and within a couple of pushes the baby was born. He came faster than the first. May 3 1982, 8:20 Monday morning our handsome prince charming came into this world. He wasn't breathing right away and the doctor left me to attend to him. When I set eyes on our son, this was the most handsome bundle of joy I had ever seen. He had a thick cap of Afro curls like his sister, straight nose and a long thin body. The first time I held him in my arms, my life began to shine. I looked into his eyes and fell in love with him like he was the only best thing in the world. We called him Junior at first and named him Roy Kataha at his baptism. That evening armed men raided the hospital. Thunder, lightning and a heavy downpour of rain didn't stop the soldiers from shouting, screaming and attacking people outside and in the hospital corridors. They went from room to room but did not see me. I believe God hid me and my baby boy protecting us from danger that night.

The next day my husband came to take us home. Soldiers were forcing us out of our house he said and because I was a foreigner he hoped I could send them away. Such attacks were common in Kampala that all one could do was pray for miracles every day. Huge, tall Northern Ugandans soldiers came to harass us day after day threatening to shoot my day old baby in my arms, literally pointing the gun towards him. I was scared and pleaded for time while my husband hid inside for fear they could kill him without hesitation. Finally we gave in, left everything behind and became homeless. I had never experienced such heartless wickedness in all my life but thank God our lives were spared. We stayed with relatives until we left to the country in Ibanda. The village was good for its fresh food and cow's milk but not for our new baby. He got a horrible attack of bronchitis and we almost lost him. His fever shot up, the breathing was a loud wheeze and there were no doctors in the village. A town clinic was a few hours away so we took the baby on a relative's motorcycle to urgent care. For nights I sat up with him, as he slept on my chest. Like any mother, every time Roy got sick I was sick with worry, crying and praying for his healing. On the other hand, he was a very smart happy-go-jolly kid. He was a charmer and every one fell in love with him at first sight. He loved his red shoes and safari suits. By two he was a comic, a good story teller and loved to sing and dance, even to Indian music. He still does it for our family fun nights.

When I traveled to India a second time with the kids, Roy was a ten month old baby. He celebrated his first and second birthday in Bangalore. He too missed his dad terribly. Once, I was reading a letter from his father who was in the UK, when he heard his name the boy ran in excitement and banged his forehead on the edge of the doorway. His aunty and I quickly rushed him to the nearest clinic. He screamed in pain and I cried all the way to the doctors. He still has a cute scar on his forehead. Another day this kid got his foot caught in a bicycle wheel when our helper was taking him to the baby sitters. He got a lot of attention from everyone. My son was too little to understand the day I was leaving for Dubai. Happily dangling his little feet through our bedroom window he was singing and waving. That was the most painful separation knowing how sick he used to get. He'd cry out for his mama and I was not there. When they escaped to India a Catholic relative took them to a shrine in Velankanni to pray for Roy's health. They shaved his head and made a vow to Mary but nothing happened. The Bible says, only Jesus died on the Cross for our salvation and for our healing. We repented of that sin of ignorance and believed God for his healing. He started kindergarten in India. For his fifth birthday in Cbennai (Madras) his dad got him a suit and a big chocolate cake.

Amusingly, when we first met in Bahrain's International airport, my beloved son had forgotten me and was calling me aunty. I missed him terribly and collected all kinds of cars, trucks and toys to surprise him. He took a long bus ride with his sister to Sacred Heart's School in Isa Town, Bahrain every day and came home with lots of stories. He turned thirteen in Bahrain before we left to Canada and ever since celebrated all his birthdays in Ontario. As newcomers from the Middle East our teenagers faced a lot of challenges but my son was good at making friends. We spent our first mother-son date in Dixie mall, shopping and eating out. We have similar tastes for spicy food and this young man is an excellent cook. Even as a boy he loved to hang out in the kitchen with his mama to help me cook and tell his long stories. On his sixteenth birthday, his sister helped surprise Roy with fifty of his school mates for a BBQ birthday party in our new Millway Gate House. He had the whole basement in our home to himself and enjoyed privacy like a king in the jungle except when we used to surprise him. On our last Niagara fall's family picnic in 2007 (the year his father passed away), he had a bicycle race with his dad and lost huffing and puffing because of his weight. But since then he's lost all his baby fat and slimmed down to a tall and handsome six footer. In many ways, he is a self made; charming and attractive young man, an achiever with potential, blessed to be a blessing! Roy is a go-getter and a risk taker like his mama.

Two days before his father passed away, Roy spent hours talking with him about marriage and real life issues. When he didn't see him in Church that Sunday, he had to go home and spend some time with his dad behind closed doors. He is a very affectionate child and has always in most occasions sneaked to take pictures alone with his mama. Being adventurous, he often stands out among his friends to do the most extra-ordinary things in life. The Lord bless him and his family; The Lord make His face to shine upon him, and be gracious to him; The Lord lift up His countenance upon him, give him peace and long life. Numbers 6:24-26. Roy Kataha is married to his beautiful wife Melanie and is an extra amazing father to his two gorgeous daughters. The Lord in His mercy and grace kept him strong and alive just for me and for Jesus' name sake. Though the enemy threatened to take his life from a day old baby and time and time again through sickness and natural teenage mistakes, I believe God's plan is bigger and brighter for my son. He will explode in all ways and continue to be a sign and wonder to the world.

This prophetic song is from the heart of a spiritually hungry boy, the Lord showed me in the spirit. He will rise as a priest, prophet, protector and provider for his home and for the Kataha clan for generations!

Since I Met You Jesus

(Song composed for Roy)

Since I Met You Jesus, my whole life has changed
Ever since I knew you, all my ways are new
And everybody tells me, I am not the same.

I don't need anybody, to make my dreams come true
You hold my hand and tell me, You make me whole and new
For Since I Met You Jesus, all I need is you.

The Reunion Baby

As a reminder of the goodness and faithfulness of our Lord Jesus, I desired for a Reunion Baby to celebrate our victory as a family. Living alone in Bahrain for three years before my husband Apollo and the two children joined me, no one believed that I had coloured children of my own except those who knew me closely. As we prayed and waited on the Lord, the following year I conceived and was expecting our third baby. It did not matter if it was a boy or a girl. Ever since the night I was saved by the Holy Spirit, something very special was happening in all our lives. I was healed of arthritis, our oldest son was delivered from bronchitis and my husband received healing from peptic ulcers. After seven years of struggles and political separation, we were happy to be alive and together again. We moved from our one room apartment to a bigger place. We had plenty of food, water and the dread of the past was fading away. We were getting ready for the next phase of our lives. Prayer does not change God but prayer changes us. We wanted God's plan in our lives.

I enjoyed being pregnant after a long break of seven years. We spoke the Word and sang to the baby in the womb. His father regularly preached to him. At thirty four I knew I was not old to carry. Sarah and Abraham's story reminded me to stop focusing on the circumstances, and to trust in God. Loving makes you smile, loving makes you cry and loving makes you forget all about time. I loved Jesus, I loved my life, and I loved my family. Up until seven months, I was doing fine. By eight months I was heavy and uncomfortable like I was carrying twins. I went into false labour and landed myself in bed for a week. It's a known fact that third pregnancy's and birth's are unpredictable and different from the first and the second. I was not afraid like the previous ones and most of all I was a Christian Believer. Nevertheless she will be saved in childbearing if they continue in faith, love, and holiness, with self-control. 1Timothy 2:15. By now I was more prepared, knowledgeable and a mother of two. Things were different in the Middle East. We had good health care, everything was readily available and we were blessed. We had no need to know the sex of the baby, we trusted God. My duties as a wife and mother did not change. I was off work, did not need a maid and had no machines to do my chores like washer dryer, dish washer, not even a microwave back then. We were young, energetic and thankful for what we had.

120

Water Baptism by Immersion

Eight months pregnant and I agreed to take my water baptism. As Christians, one of the first rites every believer should observe, either at the moment of salvation or shortly thereafter is to be baptized with water. Jesus commanded; GO ye therefore, and teach all nations, baptizing them in the name of The Father, and of The Son and of The Holy Spirit. Matthew 28:19. The word 'Baptism' means to immerse fully. It is not an option but a command. Water Baptism is a public act of obedience identifying with Christ's death, burial and resurrection as 'born again believers.' As I got out of the water this baby in my womb moved and kicked so much as if jumping for joy. I remembered John the Baptist leaped in Elizabeth's womb when she heard Mary's greeting. Luke 1:41. Water baptism by immersion does not save a person. It is only for people who have already experienced the 'new birth.' Infants and children cannot understand repentance and faith in Christ. Sprinkling of a baby would be scripturally wrong for two reasons. One, a person must be old enough to understand the commitment to Jesus Christ. Second, baptism requires full water immersion, Acts 8:38-39, John 3:23. If someone was to die before taking water baptism, their soul would still be saved. I urge you to receive this wonderful experience and desire also the 'Baptism of the Holy Spirit and Fire.' Matthew 3:11. You will enjoy heaven on earth in a whole different level of Intimacy with Jesus.

Labour pains were stronger and quicker this time. One epidural injection on my spine quickened the labour process and I was fully conscious during the process. This time the pushing was a little better than the last two and in no time my healthy baby boy was born. Today, spinal and epidural anesthesia is the most common method for painless labour. Funny thing a girl from my home town in Bangalore India helped me with the delivery. Jesse was born on July fifteenth 1989, around five thirty that Saturday evening. He was a surprise gift to all of us just in time for three of our birthdays. They thought we had the wrong baby. Jesse was very far, with a cute long nose and very straight hair unlike his older siblings. Only I knew the fact when the nurse laid him on my chest minutes after his birth, that this was our miracle, 'reunion baby!' The Lord provided every need and more for our miracle son. Our Church family came to visit us. His older siblings were excited to have a new baby brother and carried him in turns. Months later, Jesse's hair started to curl up and turned into a cute afro to everyone's amusement. He was baptized as a Catholic and later dedicated in the Full gospel Church of Philadelphia in Bahrain. In two months I miraculously got the job with the U.S. Foreign Building Office. The only hang-up was we couldn't find a safe day care. He went from to a dog lady, to a house over loaded with kids and to another until a friend helped us with his cousin who turned out to be Jesse's favourite baby sitter.

Wake up call to Husbands

Weeks after my delivery I went into postpartum depression (PPD) and for no reason I would become sad and start to weep. It can happen to any mother after child birth. During such times a woman needs care. I had no idea what was happening to me but now I learned this is a complex mix of physical, emotional, and behavioral changes that happens in a woman after child birth. After a few weeks the Lord helped me break through that depressive spirit and bounced me back to normal again. For ages no one was able to associate the after birth mood swings, emotional symptoms with depression. In the olden day's woman like me didn't understand or never talked about our feelings. Men being the silent gender left it to the women to figure out. Women need the support from their husbands and it's essential they understand this illness can impact a marriage. Some men and new fathers may feel confused, angry, worried, or frustrated. He, too, has just become a parent and may have expected this to be the best time of his life. Due to sudden changes in a woman's body, the nights up nursing, breast feeding their little bundle of joy and trying to be a normal wife and mother, depression can creep in and make her feel inadequate, helpless and weak. Gentlemen, please help your wife through it. She will need you now more than ever. Talk to her, spend time understanding her feelings and tell her you love her. Tell her you love your family, the children, the new baby and that they love her too. It's not her fault, not your fault and not the baby's fault either. Give her breaks, help share the chores, care for the baby, take the older children out for walks so she can rest and have some alone time without feeling guilty. Make sure she gets enough sleep. Encourage the mother of your children with words, hugs and appreciation. Most importantly as the priest of your home, pray together, over your wife, comfort your family and invite the joy of the Lord into your home.

Growing up, Jesse was an easy-go active little fellow. He first travelled to Bangalore India a month after he turned one. He met two of his cousins who were the same age as him; my younger sister's second son and my last brother's first daughter. Jesse was hospitalized in Bangalore for a week due to the change of weather. He was the only mixed African baby there and became everyone's friend. He had an old friend in our apartment building we called Tony Bishop because he had a small beard. This kid loved to visit Brother Tony and watch him duplicate Christian videos, children's movies and teachings to distribute to Believers on the Island. His baby sitter Patsy was his best friend that a times we had trouble bringing him home. Later he and his siblings had another friend, our Sri Lankan maid Kumadu. She loved the kids so much that she started coming to Church with us and got saved. Jesse boy loved to sing, strum on his little guitar and mimic just about anyone; his favourite Evangelists and Christian singers even in their actions. Barely three years, Jesse had a favourite yellow shirt and tie and with a comb as a microphone, he automatically became a preacher. He could repeat our Pastor's sermons and amuse everyone with his love for Jesus. Faithfully he carried his small guitar to Church every Friday and during worship he'd slowly walk up front and try to join the worship team. One morning he was playing with his building blocks in the bedroom and came running to tell me 'a man was smiling at him.' Jesse described Him in a long, brown shining robe and that he was watching him play. When he looked up, (I suppose an angel or the Lord), smiled at him and disappeared. He started kindergarten in Bahrain. Two months before his sixth birthday we traveled to Canada and by the end of our journey he made friends with most of the passengers. His high pitched voice in a funny Arab/India accent caught everyone's attention. He celebrated his seventh and the rest of his birthdays in Ontario. After his sister Belinda was married and moved out of the house, Jesse got a promotion to the basement (this was a special place where we trusted our children with responsibility and independence) which later after he got saved became his sanctuary and meeting place with God.

This cool sixteen year old teenager was challenged with real life issues like most young people face today and during this time he had an encounter with the Holy Spirit. He was touched and changed overnight! He was born-again and water baptized by immersion by his late dad, the Pastor of Believers Deliverance Church. December 2005 His father (exactly two years before he went home to be with the Lord), prophesied and transferred his mantle of anointing over Jesse in our Christmas Celebration Service by the laying on of hands and placing his jacket over him. At that time my husband had no trace of any sickness in his body. He was active, healthy, working full-time and serving the Lord and the Church part-time. All the youth were touched and baptized in the Anointing of the Holy Spirit that night. For the very first time, our sixteen year old son went under the anointing shaking, crying and speaking in tongues for over an hour. Two years later again in our Christmas Service in 2007, Jesse preached his first sermon just as his father has said. He has become a young preacher and lover of the Gospel of Jesus Christ ever since. He had a very close relationship with his dad from that night on and spent hours every day discussing the Bible with him. Their last bible discussion was just a few hours before his father's tragic death on December fourth 2007. From a youth Jesse has suffered greatly and learned some hard life lessons like all his siblings. June 2013 was the best wedding of the year. Being Jesse's mother, I had the honour to walk him down the aisle on his wedding day. That day I witnessed one of the greatest joys of my life. We had the best ever mother-son dance! Everyone, young and old danced their shoes off like David danced before the Lord. He graduated from college and this summer, 2015 Jesse graduates from York University in Toronto Canada with honours. I am so proud of my son, that he's an example as a young man to others around him in speech and conduct. 1 Timothy 4:12. Today, Jesse is blessed with a full-time job and his beautiful wife Camila who loves the Lord. Together they serve and lead worship and minister to other young people in their community and in downtown Toronto. Funny, he still plays his guitar.

The Lord is unfolding His plan in Jesse's life to lead and fight the cause of the weak and needy. Son, as you set your love upon the most high God you will reap an abundant harvest and be blessed. The Lord says to you Jesse Kataha; I will deliver you and honour you, I will set you on high, because you have known My Name. You shall call upon Me, and I will answer you: I will be with you in trouble and with long life will I satisfy you. Psalm 91. I received this song for Jesse rocking him to sleep as a baby. Because of his love for Jesus and the reverentially fear of the Lord He will carry him all the days of his life.

Quotes from Jesse Kataha

- Always remember that there are many who would long to fill your position, who would take advantage of the things you take for granted. Never forget the role you occupy, never squander the resources you live by. At the end of the day it's what you did with what you had that's of virtue not what you had because of what you did. No amount of success can compensate for failure at home. What kind of legacy will you leave behind?

- Think about this; you are destined to inherit a legacy; you are also destined to leave one. Will the nature of your legacy embody serenity and tranquility or chaos and conflict?

- Character can be measured by the type of behaviour you conduct towards those who can do nothing for you.

- In a society where consumerism predominantly captivates the human will, may we never become desensitized to practicing generosity.

- We don't obey to be accepted, we are accepted therefore we obey.

A Drop of His Blood

(*Song composed for Jesse*)

Even a drop of His blood can make a difference
Even a drop of His blood can set you free
My Jesus, He died on Calvary to pardon and sanctify me.

What a marvelous price, He paid for you and me
My Jesus my Lord and my King.
Jesus suffered and died to set all men free
My Redeemer, my Lord and my King.

Even a drop of His blood can make a difference
Even a drop of His blood can set you free
My Jesus, He died on Calvary to pardon and sanctify me.

You can Choose Your Baby's Sex

We were a happy, blessed, fortunate, prosperous and a busy family, both with full time jobs in Bahrain, holding cell groups, prayer and deliverance sessions in our home and ministering to others. By this time, our oldest daughter was thirteen, the big son a pre-teen and our third boy was five. I missed out three years of my daughter Belinda's life so I felt entitled to having a second baby girl. Besides, a couple in our Church, also a part of our cell meetings had a pretty baby daughter and I loved Zeeni. Soon I was pregnant again. As the months got closer, the Lord gave us the name 'Rachel' and we were excited and held on to that by faith. Friends at work were amused that I could choose my baby's sex. I did not need an ultrasound to believe for our miracle baby girl. This gave me an opening to share my faith and to pray for others. I took the Bible literally. It was God speaking, I was His daughter asking for my heart's desires and I believed He heard me. Ask and it shall be given to you. Matthew 7:7. And whatsoever ye shall ask in my name, that will I do, that the Father may be glorified in the Son. John 14:13-14. So many supernatural miracles happened in our lives before and I trusted this would be easy to receive. My whatsoever was my baby girl. The Christian faith is all about believing in a God greater than everyone and everything else. For most couples, the odds of predicting the gender of their child are roughly the same as flipping a coin. We were old school and loved surprises.

When you believe and actually receive the miracle in your hands it can blow your mind in awe and this happens to me even today. No technology, old wives tales, bedroom possibilities can match the great Creator of all. For ages, man has complicated everything and tried to by-pass God. Why the world is confused because they deny the existence of the Great I AM. They'd rather believe in horoscope, the moon and technology but not the living Word of God who was from the beginning of time. He also created time. John 1:1-2. The first choice in the Garden of Eden still harasses man today and yet we never get it. You can wait passively, or expectantly. A passive person hopes something good will happen and is willing to sit around waiting and after a short time they give up. The expectant person is hopeful because they believe in the God of miracles and they can receive miracles every day.

Pregnancy and Parenthood

Having a baby is the most exciting time in any woman's life and a fourth one for me was more exciting. After God created Adam and Eve He blessed them. Genesis 1:22, 28. When we trust Him in all things, we can embrace parenthood and be a blessing to others and to our children. The Lord appeared to Jacob and declared a blessing on him that we too can receive for generations. God said to him, I am God Almighty. Be fruitful and multiply; a nation and a company of nations shall come from you and kings shall be born of your stock. Genesis 11:35. A child is a blessing to a parent, a new soul that did not exist before and a gift entrusted to us for a life time. Enjoy the early years of parenthood, babies grow up quickly and will soon be adults ready to leave your nest. A mother's love does not stop at eight, eighteen or fifty eight. The best thing to do for your children is to let them to do things for themselves, and grow up strong to experience life on their own. Allow them to take the bus, subway and to walk. They will be better people you will be proud of. You know for sure your children has grown up when they stop asking you where they came from and refuse to tell you where they're going. We cannot always build the future for our youth but we sure can build our youth for the future.

Today there are too many questions and people like to pry into every little detail before and during pregnancy. Why as soon as they see a defect they're ready to kill, abort the baby not realizing that is a life, a whole human being. High tech and modern medicine has not only taken the joy out of pregnancy but has caused confusion and fear. In our day, seldom we went for check-ups except if there was a need and towards the final months. We lived happy, busy lives and by instinct, according to our gut feelings brought up some great, healthy children. Pregnancy symptoms were normal to us and as months went by and we developed taste for special foods and attention. We used home remedies for everything like the common colds, stomach aches, bruises, etc., and we ate healthy. The U.S. Embassy in Manama gave me a baby shower before I went on maternity leave with a big cake, compliments from Hilton hotel. Some of those friends are still in contact with me today and are amazed with this testimony.

God-Sent Angels

With my fourth baby I was truly blessed. I was surrounded and blessed with God-sent angels to assist me. Nurses from my women's bible study group were on duty that day. Two of them assisted me with special care and made me feel comfortable. The epidural injecting to help reduce the pain did its trick again and in a few hours with one contraction the baby was born. I guess the fourth baby is quicker and easier than the others. But I believe it was because Jesus was in my life and He made all things beautiful. My promised gift and the baby girl I asked and believed God for made her grand entrance into this world with a lot of attention! She was so beautiful! Our precious Rachel was born on May twenty first 1994, Saturday around eleven in the morning. In the Middle East, due to the Arab Muslim culture men are not allowed in the birthing ward so my husband waited outside for the good news. He came in an hour later and was excited beyond words. She was the first baby he carried within an hour of her birth. Our Pastor and his wife visited us later that evening along with other friends and Sister Carol lifted the baby up and prophesied calling out 'Rachel Ruth!' So we named her Rachel Ruth Kataha. She was the fairest, cutest baby doll face with a scanty Afro and a cute flat nose to mark the Kataha brand. All her siblings loved their little baby sister and were delighted to carry her. Belinda was the biggest helper and a proud big sister. Her brothers Roy was boasting about his little sister with pride and especially Jesse became over-protective trying to shield her from anyone kissing her. The whole Church family loved Rachel and she went from hand to hand. She was a very special gift sent to complete our family. There was no greater joy! The Lord supernaturally provided each and everything we needed for this baby; she the best clothes, supply of diapers, (O yes Rachel and Jesse both wore diapers in Bahrain), the best baby products and essentials we needed. We did not have to buy a thing for months. She is the most blessed child even today.

We travelled to Canada a day after Rachel's first birthday. From her second year on she celebrated all her birthdays in Canada. Her dada was the best baby sitter during the day and played in her dolls house and watched her TV programs with her. He worked at nights and we exchanged car keys at the door because we couldn't trust anyone else to take care of our children. Her Mama was always her special friend and story teller. Times she'd ride her bicycle to school in the summers and her dad would follow her from a distance to see that his little girl was safe. Her first date with her father was when he took her to Pickle Barrel on her thirteenth birthday. Rachel was good in basketball, music, interpretive dance and drama. She played the keyboard in our Church from young as eleven years old. Midst all the sorrows, losses and trials of our family she has grown into one beautiful and strong young adult. Just like Esther she was born for such a time, a life for a divine purpose.

This girl loves adventure and has traveled to many countries already. We ministered together on our mission's trip to Bahrain and she led worship. Many young people were touched by the Holy Spirit during these meetings and were delivered and renewed. We visited the home where we lived, Salmaniya hospital she was born in, our favourite Marina Park and also strolled about in the scorching heat in the Bab el-Bahrain Souq (malls and shopping center) in Manama. We went by the Marina Club where her father worked and the U.S. Embassy in Zinc Bahrain. In Melbourne she dared to go on a jet plane with her aunt. We took a sightseeing tour to the Twelve Apostles Great Ocean, and saw all the beautiful attractions. We drove by Sydney and toured the Opera House and Arts Center and lots of other places. One of Rachel's dreams was to attend the Hill Song Church and watch their live worship in Sydney Australia. She got her first car in Michigan and her step father Fred was her driving instructor. She has a love for fashion and drama. By heart she is a Canadian!

Get ready Rachel; you will have more dreams than memories, more opportunities than chances, more hard work than luck and more friends than acquaintances. Live a life of thanksgiving, cherish the moments, hold on to wisdom, speak out your dreams and rejoice in the now. Love fearlessly, forgive easily, smile heartily, laugh at your wrongs, sing to the heavens and dance in the rain. Reach for the stars girl, look for that silver lining and hide in the presence of Jehovah, He will never let you down. Enjoy life in Christ! Know, see and dream big, the best is yet to come. Proud of my princess daughter Rachel Ruth Kataha! Who would have thought of this day but the Lord? To see you venture into a brand new, awesome and exciting tomorrow. Rachel has grown into one beautiful, brave, exciting, determined, glowing daughter of the King. Keep it up girl and be proud of yourself.

Loving memories from Rachel!

Quote; it's not just on Mother's Day that I stop and think how lucky I am to have you. Seems like every day comes with blessings that can be traced back to you ---from chances to use the lessons you've taught, to memories of times we've shared ---there's so much that reminds me of you and your love. Thank you, Mom, for everything. I'll always be grateful for you. Happy Mother's Day! Love you forever and always, my Mama you'll always be! Rae. *End Quote*

I Belong to Jesus

(*Song composed for Rachel*)

I belong to Jesus, am the heir to His throne
Am a Royal Priesthood
Just because I belong to Him.

Jesus calls me His beloved, He even calls me friend
He said He'll never leave me
Just because I belong to Him.

He says He loves me, He even died for me
He's building my mansion
And He'll come and take me home.

A Mother's Love

It's heartbreaking and a scary thing to hear your child that you carried for nine months curse you and say; 'I hate you' and other mean things. After all the sleepless nights with a crying baby, worrisome days with a sick child, tedious conflicts with a lost teenager, through all the struggles of life and looking out for their future, it comes down to this, disrespect and rebellion. A mother can be at risk spiritually, emotionally, and physically if she doesn't take care of herself during these stressful trials. Sadly, I've been through this and it tries to creep in every once in a while. Fortunately, prayer is the only answer. If you're not praying for your child in faith, then who will? Our enemy, Satan, seeks to discourage and weaken our faith just as He did to Eve. With Patience you will persevere through this season of trial as well. God hears your prayers and honors them. Speak His word daily and encourage yourself in the Lord. We as mothers have the unique calling to stay on our knees and face in weeping intercession for our children until we take our last breath. There will be great joy around the throne of Jesus Christ when we see a generation of our children blessed by our unceasing and relentless prayers. The acronym L-O-V-E is to encourage the worn-out mom to know that she is loved and cherished by her heavenly Father. The Lord will carry you through.

L - Listen to God's direction in prayer and meditation. He will give you wisdom and insight to not only help your child, but give you strength to keep moving forward.

O - Open your heart to forgiveness, Colossians 3:13. Seek God's comfort and forgive so you can love them without bitterness. They are sinning against God and will have to give an account one day. Whoever curses his father or his mother, his lamp will be put out… Proverbs 20:20

V - Value this season of trial as an opportunity for you and your child. We would never be prayer warrior intercessors if it wasn't for our children. Stay connected to the vine. John 15:4-5.

E - Expect the Lord to move in His purpose and timing. There is hope in your future, says the Lord that your children shall come back to their own border. Jeremiah 31:17. Believe and receive!

Parenting Tips:

If you are doing all in the natural to please your kids, what legacy, inheritance, memories and blessings are you leaving them behind? How will they set the standard high when they look for their own spouses and families? Train up a child in the way he should go, and when he is old he will not depart from it. Proverbs 22:6. Everything else will pass away but what they see you do and hear you say will never leave their memory. There is no greater joy, no better gift or greater blessing than to see your Children walk, serve and love Christ, because when all is said and done, they will have eternity to hold on to. We may not be there to see it but we can rest to know they are blessed down to a thousand generations. Exodus 20:6. Every time I dropped my children off to school, to the mall, youth meetings or just anywhere, I learned to speak over their lives and say; 'be blessed to be a blessing!' Now they say it to their children. This was God's promise to Abraham who is the father of faith. The word 'blessed' means to be happy, fortunate, prosperous and enviable. I will make you a great nation; I will bless you and make your name great; and you shall be a blessing I will bless those who bless you, and I will curse him who curses you; and in you all the families of the earth shall be blessed. Even from a distance you can touch, reach out and love your children the best you know how.

Behold, children are a heritage from the Lord,
The fruit of the womb a reward.

As arrows are in the hand of a warrior,
so are the children of one's youth.

Happy, blessed, and fortunate is the man
whose quiver is filled with them!

They will not be put to shame when they speak with their adversaries

[in gatherings] at the [city's] gate.

Psalm 127:3-5

Chapter Seven

It is good to preach stories from the Bible, but it's another thing to preach, teach and declare your real life story through the Bible. Unless you have lived it, walked it, witnessed it and come through it no one knows the Resurrection Power of the Holy Spirit better than one who depends on it from day to day. This is walking in Intimacy! Living may be easy, dying to live takes courage. Even more, daring to expose evil and glorious to shout on every mountaintop that our Jesus Christ is forever Lord! The Holy Spirit boldness will stir up the lion in you to fight for your life, your marriage, your children, your health and for your sanity! This narrow path is getting narrower, the battles hotter but the victory is sweeter. We shall rejoice and sing for the Lord is good and His mercies endure forever!

Our move to Ontario was a blessing and a fulfillment of the promise of God in 1989. As a young family of six, we were excited, bursting with energy to dive in and plunge into a completely new world. Friends housed us for a few days and then we moved into a motel until we found a three bedroom apartment in the city. The move to Canada was our biggest life saver; we had no country, no home and nowhere else we'd rather be than in the will of God. The Lord provided for our travel and a large sum of money that was required to enter the country. He promised to bring us into a land flowing with milk and honey. The initial years were difficult but at least we were together as a family. We worked at odd jobs to make ends meet: stuffing envelopes, washing floors, scammed by agents and the usual stories that go along with new immigrants. I sold natural gas door to door, falling in the heavy snowfall with my walking shoes. I got lost in the dark and angels led me home a couple of times.

This should be on video as it seems funny now but not back then. My husband and I shared the chores, babysitting, picking and dropping kids and the rest. No one understood from where and how far the Kataha family had already come.

Any newcomer will tell of the challenges one faces in a large family with small children trying to adapt to the weather and high standard of living in Canada. Everything was new to us; we needed Canadian experience no matter how qualified one is, to speak in a certain style (funny, we already had a mixed Anglo-India-African and Arab accent), make new friends and to deal with teenagers who were suddenly thrown into a society of competition, peer-pressure and discrimination. We won some and lost in some areas. It took sacrifice, hard work and lots of encouragement between us, so our children could enjoy better lives than we did growing up. We tried everything to keep the home fires burning. My husband Apollo worked twelve hours at night while I held the fort during the day and exchanged one set of car keys at the door and thank God for everything. I worked, trained, picked up and dropped off the kids, cooked, cleaned as a usual housewife, mother and home maker. We got low on our savings due to ministry and family obligations. Three months after our arrival, my husband was led to go evangelize to his people and country in Uganda. We worked for minimum wage and landed in the 'Food Bank' for a few weeks, received food boxes and warm clothing from friends we made in Church. I believe the Lord was teaching us how to receive in humility. Once I was led to ask a Pastor's wife for food from her freezer and she said, 'she was going to pray about it.' She never got back to me. That too was a lesson well learned. We, the whole family woke up very early each morning to pray in our tiny Bethlehem Prayer Room and the Lord was beginning to show us His promises of abundance. We held on to them, confessed them every day and nothing was going to shake our walk with Jesus. Now to Him Who, by (in consequence of) the [action of His] power that is at work within us, is able to [carry out His purpose and] do superabundantly, far over and above all that we [dare] ask or think [infinitely beyond our highest prayers, desires, thoughts, hopes, or dreams]-To Him be glory in the church and in Christ Jesus throughout all generations forever and ever. Amen (so be it). Ephesians 3:20-21. That same year, our son Jesse came home with a package from school, an anonymous lady bought him a brand new snow suit and boots. For Christmas, we received two turkeys, two bags of potatoes, warm clothing and gifts for the children. We worked hard, loved hard and served the Lord with all our hearts.

To Receive and to Give

One of the hardest lessons for a Christian is learning to receive in humility and to give without boasting. Man by nature is born with pride. People like to make a show in their giving by works. For years when I was alone without my family in Bahrain, many prominent folks in the Catholic Church tried to help me. I appreciated those who sincerely blessed me in many ways but there were some who embarrassed me like a hopeless, abandoned beggar without her 'black' husband and made me an exhibit of pity. That is the religious world we live in today but thank God for His amazing grace. Jesus showed up and showed us off by rescuing, restoring and prospering us beyond our wildest dreams. Those same people became jealous and never wanted to talk to me after the family was reunited. From our experiences we learned to make our home an open sanctuary for others in need. We gave away everything we had in Bahrain and looked for opportunities to bless others. But we had to learn hard how to receive too. It's pretty humbling to receive from the people God places around us, but He broke our pride and helped us overcome in that area too.

Learning to receive love can also be difficult for some; they have been hurt too many times and struggle to even trust God. For this reason, we as Believers need to develop a safe environment for fellowship and trust. Where the broken hearted and hurting can come and bask in unconditional love so they too can trust God like us. Never forget that our actions speak louder than words. One of the beliefs today is, "better to give than to receive." The focus on tithing and "giving" has been the tune so loud in Church and on the TV that makes some feel guilty and stop going to church. It makes no logical sense to me. To give requires someone to receive. All my life, I have practiced giving religiously even while I had need and longing to receive. No one ever taught me how to receive. I always feel the need to give something in return. I wave people away from helping me in a grocery line, no matter what I am dropping. When we begin to examine this, we see that receiving involves vulnerability and we feel less as a receiver. When we give, we feel in charge. Giving and receiving go hand-in-hand. Just the other day when we dropped into a store after Church, we noticed a woman short of money to pay her bill. The Lord impressed in our hearts to 'give'. The tears and hugs were unimaginable, even the cashier came for a hug. This opened a door to share Jesus openly right there and then and many had eyes to see and ears to hear the sweet name of our Lord Jesus. Receiving is a learned skill. I can accept a gift with a "thank you" instead of jumping up to return the favor. It's nice to let others help with grace and be grateful that someone wants to be of service. Time we let others have the fun of giving too and we can learn to receive and enjoy our blessings.

In time, after a few years of hard work and prayer, the Lord was beginning to show off our blessings. We worked steady jobs and bought our first home from where we started our open-house ministry in Canada. My highly qualified husband was forced to temporarily take up work in a General Motors factory and got stuck there for ten years due to financial pressures. After a few years from a labourer doing dirty jobs, he was promoted to a machine operator. The discrimination and humiliation he endured caused God to do something supernatural in his favour. In the meantime he was sharing the Gospel and bringing many souls to Jesus and into the Church. The factory changed supervisors who recognized his hard work and to everyone's amazement, they raised him up as a plant Engineer (he was not qualified in this field) and got the highest pay. Promotion does come from the east or the west but from the Lord. Psalm 75:6. He trained others until he resigned to serve full-time in ministry. I worked for the U.S. Consulate in Toronto, as well as jobs closer to home and wound up with the Benny Hinn Ministries in Mississauga. I later assisted my husband as an Administrator and Co-Pastor for our BDM Church.

The healing and deliverance ministry followed us from Bahrain way before we started the Church. By word of mouth people started contacting us. Some came to visit and during prayer or in the course of our conversation suddenly someone would manifest with evil spirits. Discerning how severe the case may be, we would have to put it off for fasting and prayer or right there begin to pray and carry out deliverance. Once, a friend brought three of her sisters visiting from Dubai to pray for her niece who was starting university. While we were praying and anointing the girl, her mother started manifesting in a man's voice and gave us a history of his entry and possession of the entire family. Much of it was true but some lies, just like the lying nature of the devil. After praying for the daughter, we began to minister to the oppressed woman. This took till two in the morning until we poured a bottle of anointing oil over her head and she was finally loosed by the power of the blood and Name of Jesus. We're all ordained by God to deliver others in one way or another, spiritually, socially, materially or physically. As Believers we are given a full package of authority when we first get saved which includes healing the sick and casting out demons. Mark 16:17-18. Today deliverance ministry is almost unheard of because it is challenged on the battle front and can only survive with continuous fasting prayer and intercession. Most Churches get busy with programs and the people are still oppressed and remain in bondage.

Believers Deliverance Ministries (BDM)

My husband Apollo and I founded the Believers Deliverance Ministries in Canada. This Church was birthed in the basement of our home in November 2000 and a year later we relocated to the city's Community Center. The great commission of Jesus Christ is to go and make disciples of all nations. Matthew 28:16-20. We were ordained Evangelists from Bahrain who answered the call to usher in the presence of the Holy Spirit so people can receive divine healing and be set free from demonic oppression. Jesus said, And as you go, preach, saying, The Kingdom of Heaven is at hand, "Heal the sick, cleanse the Lepers, raise the dead, cast out demons. Freely you have received, freely give." Matthew 10:7-8. Christian deliverance means that God wants to rescue someone from their chains of bondage, oppression, hardship, or domination by evil and restore them with His righteousness, peace and joy. It Is the Holy Spirit who brings deliverance and we were His instruments. We had a multicultural Church of people from over ten different nations including local Canadians; men and women of all faiths as well as Muslim and Hindu converts. People came from all over seeking release from hearing voices, addictions, emotional trauma due to past hurts and abuses, and many other forms of spiritual bondage. We held Bible studies and Intercessory Prayer way before the ministry officially began. The Lord gave me Woman Ablaze early in that year and we took off with open-house monthly breakfasts and many were being touched, healed and saved (some in that order). We had out outreach programs, youth gatherings and a food bank to help newcomers, single moms and seniors in the Community. Many of those precious are even serving the Lord today. One Hindu convert amazingly grew rapidly in the Lord and became our Missions Director for the Caribbean Islands. Later Brother Bill carried the Gospel to his home town in Trinidad and started his own ministry before he went home to be with Jesus.

We have seen demon possession; all kinds of oppression and fears manifest and torment God's people. We have taught and encouraged people to walk in holiness and in the fear of the Lord. You must close doors to demonic entry and keep your home and vessel clean. Places like casinos, bars, strip clubs, temples and worshipping of idols, even praying to the dead and keeping charms and omens in the house can give the enemy a foothold. These evil spirits will harass and even sexually abuse you or your children (like many cases we've delivered) if you are not discerning and prayerful. Your marriage can suffer demonic attack if you open doors also out of curiosity. Many feel drained, tired and have issues in their marriage bed due to oppression. Babies, little children and pets can be tormented by evil spirits. Fear not! God has not given us a spirit of fear but has given us His Resurrection Power of the Holy Spirit, the Agape Love of Abba Father and a Sound, disciplined mind of Jesus Christ. 2 Timothy 1:7. If fear is tormenting you today, confess this scripture with your name in it and speak it out loud. Print, write out the different promises of God and post them on your walls where you and your children can have ready access. Deuteronomy 11:18-23, Joshua 1:8. Use your authority in the name of Jesus and put on the whole armour of God. Ephesians 6:10-18. A Christian home must have a spiritual house cleaning, room to room and get rid of soul ties or idols in any form.

Testimony of Late Husband, Apollo Kataha

I Will Destroy Your Body! "February 8th 2006 I was admitted to hospital with an aneurysm of the artery behind my right knee. It developed from an untreated blood clot that got infected. I cried out for more than five hours in excruciating pain before the surgery. When I came out of anesthesia I was coughing blood and my chest hurt. They did a by-pass with an artificial insertion on my leg and I spent the next six days in hospital. Two months later, I felt the same unbearable pain again but this time it was worse. I passed out at home when my wife and son prayed and I recovered for a little while. They immediately rushed me to emergency. After a vascular test they found the same problem. The three inch insertion caused more infection, swelling and spread causing my life in danger. I had to undergo another surgery. This time they would have to remove a twelve inch vein from the other leg and by-pass it into the infected one. I was immediately transferred to Toronto General Hospital to see the top surgeons. The cardiac vascular surgeon after examining me said my condition was complicated and serious. There was a possibility of losing my leg or life itself. He was going to wait for the next four days unless the artery ruptured. After taking several ultrasound and tests to prepare me for the by-pass, he called in more surgeons to assist. Till the last minute they could not find the much needed vein.

That night before surgery, my surgeon came to talk to me and looked concerned. But as he left he said, "Mr. Apollo if God smiles on you and on us may be all will be fine". That was the only word I wanted to hear at that time and I felt strengthened. I answered back; "Yes Sir, indeed God will smile on me and on you." Till now I had not considered the possibility of death. I could not understand whether this was the time for me to go home to the Lord. I thought about my wife, the children especially my youngest daughter Rachel, who was almost twelve years old at that time. I did not want to leave them. I despaired in fear. That night I spent a lot of time praying for a miracle. Somehow I believed I would wake up totally healed and wouldn't need the surgery. In the morning I realized that did not happen and they came to take me for surgery. Around nine thirty my wife kissed me a 'God bless' and it almost seemed I would never see her again, like it was my final journey as they wheeled me in. I started speaking to God in my heart, "Lord I surrender to you right now. If this is the time, Lord receive my spirit. But if you still have work for me in this world I am sure You will bring me back to life." Later I understood that at the last minute they discovered a usable vein two inches longer than the desired length. It was however deep and instead of the usual half an hour to get it out, they took three hours. During that time I bled profusely. An attempt to trap the blood in my stomach created serious circulation problems and my heart stopped. Doctors panicked trying to reinstate the heart beat and it was another six and half hours to complete the surgery. Due to complications I had taken a longer time to recover and another three hours to come out of anesthesia. The whole day till late that night my wife waited, crying and praying all alone. Close to ten a Church Elder and his wife came and accompanied her and took her home. I vaguely recollect when she came into the recovery room before leaving, kissed me and had to return the next day. She stayed with me the rest of the nights, taking a train back and forth to care for the children, the house and the Church."

Death and Hell Experience, by Late Apollo Kataha

During my state of unconsciousness (temporary death), I entered into a place no one, not even your greatest enemy should go to. It is very hard to describe. I was caught up in something that looked like a huge egg and

I could not escape. Trapped inside this thing, I had no hope of coming out. I felt like a little bird caught up in between huge scary, filthy and extremely enormous figures, freaky looking creatures and of all shapes and sizes. Everything was sharply colourful with different flash colors that badly hurt my eyes. All these weird and freaky figures and scary monstrous creatures moved nonstop coming towards me. They came at lightning speed from every direction, all at once and I screamed continuously in terror. Sharp objects were flying from everywhere and coming into me one after another. Then I saw a very scary sight, greasy thick steaming smog looked like clouds mingled with flames of fire. Extremely terrifying giant size beasts I have never seen before together with huge freaky looking people with very long hair, coloured bodies and long, sharp teeth were all coming at top speed at me. Each time I thought this was the end; more weird figures and beastly creatures of all shapes and sizes showed up to torment and terrify me, like this was never going to end. Nonstop I was screaming and crying hopelessly, but no one could hear me. It seemed that all these smells, sights, sounds and tastes were coming into me and went through my body to torment me as I screamed in extreme fear and pain. All my senses, every opening in my body was tormented at busting point and without any relief. Suddenly I popped out of this egg like thing and heard myself say, "Who would want to come here? This is hell!"

From here, I stepped into a big open ground and was confronted by a young girl of about eight years old, dressed in a small white top and naked from the waist down. I perceived this was an evil spirit and she said to me "I have come to destroy your body". I replied "You have no right to destroy me. I am the temple of the Holy Spirit and only God can destroy me." She insisted she was going to destroy me because there was sin in my life. I looked at 'it' and declared, "You are a lying spirit and there's no sin in my life. If my body is defiled only then can God allow you to do that." She persisted 'there was sin' in me. So I asked, "What sin do you convict me of? She replied 'there's adultery in you' mentioning the name of a Pastor's wife I know, but have not seen for over twelve years. I laughed, "That's my sister, I said." and the spirit disappeared. I wondered about the meaning of this entire experience. Immediately I became aware that this was the accusation of adultery and sexual immorality in the Body of Christ. The Church today is in spiritual adultery and needs to repent. I discerned that the spirit of Jezebel is and will target the Church more violently in the last days; to destroy Pastors, Leaders, and Elders of the Church Body. The Lord protected my life that day and I live to tell this story and to warn the Body of Christ for what's coming.

I woke up in intensive care and the first question I asked the nurse was, "do I still have both my legs?" She said, "Yes, both your legs are there." I started thanking the Lord in my heart that He had actually raised me from the dead. They said I may require a longer time to recover, at least six months in rehab. A week later I was discharged. I received home care for several months and in a month's time I was able to walk with a cane. During this time my wife served as the senior Pastor, taking care of me, the home and the Church. Being a woman, she faced a lot of challenges and resistance from the leaders in our Church. The same Jezebel spirit was at work causing discord and division among the brethren. Three months later I returned and two of our elders suddenly left the church without a reason. One was afraid when he saw my twelve inch zipper wounds on both legs and didn't think I would live. He was in shock to see me walking again. The other was not happy to see me back. A few others were made to stumble. My wife and I being in the deliverance ministry for long discerned this spirit of Jezebel and waged war against 'it' in fasting and intercessory prayer. At the same time my wife was doing a teaching on this topic in her women's home group. God was releasing a fresh anointing and souls were added to the church. I began to walk with the cane for a while until I was completely healed and went back to my normal activities. To God be all the glory!"

My husband shared this testimony with most of our congregation. With great wisdom he began to prepare us spiritually, emotionally and financially and he himself started doing things differently. We continued to believe God for his total recovery. I was scanning through files on his laptop after his death and surprisingly came across this praise report. I felt it was needful to share with the Family and the Body of Christ as an evidence and testimony to my book the Lord impressed on my heart "I Cheated Death" for the glory of His name!

Death is like an Amputation

Death rips apart a piece of you. Like an amputation and the pain never really goes away! We celebrated BDM's seventh anniversary on November fourth 2007. A day earlier my husband officiated the wedding of our Ghanaian Deacon and his beautiful Brazilian wife. We left the reception early because he was in great pain. The Holy Spirit led me into a place of prayer and intercession in the weeks that followed and I was troubled in my spirit. After the death of both our mothers, I had no idea that death was coming to my house again. Six months before had we travelled to Uganda for his mother's funeral. We transitioned in the UK, met his Ghanaian colleague and best friend who studied in India with him and acted as his spokesperson before we got married. He made the journey through a lot of difficulty. Together we prayed about this uneasiness in our spirits and talked about sensitive issues. The Sunday before he passed away he wanted to stay home and pray. He anointed me with holy oil and released me to preach the Word as he always does. The swelling on his knee was increasing and he was limping but refused to go to the hospital saying 'God has to heal me or take me.' That evening we watched a Laurel and Hardy comedy on his laptop and laughed together for the last time. The next day, he hurriedly finished up the reconstruction of our basement and we conducted a marriage counseling session till ten in the night. Later we sat down for family prayer and discussed the Bible till late after which he went into his sanctuary and spent time in prayer till early morning.

Before leaving to drop my daughter off to school that Tuesday, I sent my son with his father's breakfast and they talked about the anointing; I think it was about Samson. I hurriedly came home to tend to my husband and found him sitting up in bed waiting for me. He was smiling at me from ear to ear and looked so joyful, I have never seen him so happy like this before and thought he was trying to tease me. I tried to help him out of bed and suddenly the aneurysm behind his right knee ruptured and he bled all over. I felt terribly helpless that I could not stop the bleeding and panicked. Knowing how I was always scared to see blood, he shouted out 'call 911' and collapsed on the bed. I screamed out for Jesse (thank God he was home) and he came running upstairs to help me. I called the emergency line, phoned my daughter to pick up her babies and jumped on the bed to give him mouth to mouth resuscitation. I felt desperately helpless. All of a sudden while my son was still holding his father's leg, he opened his eyes and lifted himself half way from the bed and stared into Jesse's face, for a whole minute. I froze looking from one to the other and knew something too sacred and special was happening here. As if he was conveying a message to his son, he then collapsed again and never recovered after that. The two of us will never forget that moment. After

Jesse's supernatural conversion two years eaerlier, he and his father were inseparable and spent hours discussing the word almost every night. No one understands the spiritual bond between a father and a child especially with his sons and one who was spiritually tuned to his earthly father and heavenly Father. It's not the same as mother and child. I pray men will learn and understand how much a godly father can impact the lives of his children for generations. Let us pass on the Baton of our Faith to our children's children's children so they can courageously run this race with boldness, even after we have left this world. Hear, my sons, the instruction of a father, and pay attention in order to gain and to know intelligent discernment, comprehension, and interpretation [of spiritual matters]. For I give you good doctrine [what is to be received]; do not forsake my teaching. When I was a son with my father...He taught me and said to me, Let your heart hold fast my words; keep my commandments and live.. Proverbs 13:22. As a wife and a mother this was the most precious moment of my life. For this reason the enemy has tried hard to bring discord and strife in our family and to silence me from speaking out the truth. This is the intimidating controlling spirit of Jezebel who is afraid of the next generation of prophets who like Jeremiah will speak the word of the Lord with boldness and will destroy the works of Satan and hell.

By the time the paramedics arrived my dear husband bled over 80 percent, lost oxygen to his brain and was almost dead. They sent us out of the room and the police started investigations. It happened all too fast and we were all in shock. We followed the ambulance to and waited in the intensive care lounge for a long time until I insisted to see him. He lay there lifeless with tubes running all over his body. His feet were cold. I hugged his face and kissed him saying, 'Darling, you are going to make it; you will be healed in Jesus name.' Then I heard someone say, 'he won't make it' and I lost control. I started crying, praying and preaching at the same time commanding him to come back to life. They rushed him for surgery. While a doctor was explaining to us about the possibility of amputation, another came behind and shook his head saying, "He did not make, he has passed away!" How does a woman handle the death of a man she spent almost twenty nine years of her life with and been through so much together, both good and bad? I suddenly felt alone and my feet gave way. The vows we made 'till death do us part' was painful now that they became reality to me. No one yet knows how to face death, it's like you want to die too. But then we grieve with a hope of seeing our loved ones again someday but at that time nothing makes sense. The Comforter quickened my spirit to go and release him. I believed this was for my own sake and for my children who did not know then how to react. We all went in, held hands around the body and prayed. "O Father God, You gave and You took our dada, blessed be Your Name Jesus forever. We don't know how we will make it from here but we trust in You." Thank God, He gives extraordinary strength at the right time. Although we are given power and authority to raise the dead and God is able to heal completely, in this case it would be selfish of us. He was already brain dead and would be a vegetable in a wheel chair for the rest of his life. That is not a good testimony. So we surrendered completely to the Sovereignty of God and prayed for more grace.

Grief like Fear Pangs

No one ever told me that grief felt like fear. I was not afraid, but the sensation was like being afraid. The same flutter in my stomach, the restlessness and the emptiness remained. "I once read, 'I lay awake all night with a headache, thinking about the headache and about lying awake.' This is so true in life. Part of every misery is, the fact that you don't merely suffer but have to keep on thinking about the fact that you suffer. I not only lived each endless day in grief, but lived thinking how to live each day, in grief. For in grief nothing is the same. One keeps on emerging from a reoccurring phase, round and round; up one day and down the other. It simply makes you numb. I cannot remember all that happened that day, but I know this was a vicious attack of the enemy against our ministry, family and individual lives. After everyone left, the children and I held each other and cried out like babies. None of us knew how to comfort each other. Though I tried so hard even I failed as a mother to understand what each one of my darling children were going through at that time and in the days, weeks and years that followed. That night as I lay in bed numb, I prayed for strength. Then 'something' walked into the room and came on my bed and lay on top of me. I froze and could not move. I tried to scream 'the blood, the blood' but no sound came. I felt a cold chill go through my body and I knew well that this was a familiar spirit trying to mimic my husband. In my heart I was calling out the name of "Jesus" and finally I got loose and screamed out 'in Jesus name get out you lying spirit I know where my husband is. He is in heaven and the blood of Jesus against you!' A smell of blood was still in the room even though our young people tried to clean up and threw the carpet out. The next day was the funeral service and people came from everywhere. So many who knew their friend, brother and Pastor Apollo, from his workplace, our community, neighbourhood, school principal, the Church family and friends came to support us. My husband was only fifty two years old; we were the same age just two days apart. Our youngest daughter was barely thirteen. Both my sons, our Mentor Pastor McGuire and a friend from Bahrain made their speeches and my oldest daughter sang her favourite song to honour her father. Jesse's speech shook everyone, he said; 'hell will pay for this day!' This was one of the saddest days of all our lives.

I dreaded when the house was empty, going shopping only to reach out for his favourite foods and suddenly I leave my shopping cart and run out to sit and weep in my car. The agony of each night in an empty bed hoping it never happened, thinking he will return one day. Yet it was true, my husband was dead and gone, leaving me all alone. To face this reality each day was cruel. There was no one to talk, to walk this lonely journey with me except the Holy Spirit. Being a Pastor and a Minister's wife was the worst. I suffered great loneliness. Now it was me needing ministry, support, help and I had none. I couldn't dress, eat, walk or cry any more. I was absolutely miserable. Those who tried still didn't know the extent of my pain. How does one put grief into words and what can comfort a brokenhearted soul anyway? There was no reason to question, because death comes to everyone. Of course it is different when it happens to you, not in imagination but in reality. The children tried to pretend and avoided talking about their feelings because they thought I was already handling a lot. Days that followed were both utterly full and completely empty. Full of responsibilities and activity and yet empty of life. Death is never easy, yet we all have to face it someday. Its true one can have great faith to pray for healing, miracles and a long life. Yet 'death' can happen to anyone. Precious in the eyes of Lord Jehovah is the death of His righteous people. Psalm 116:15. We are told in scripture that 'blessed are they that mourn,' I could accept that, but not when it happened to me. The only hope was that he was in no more pain and I knew that too well how he used to weep like a child and cry out in agony and I would weep with him, hold him close and pray for the Holy Spirit to comfort his body and mind. I was beginning to thank God for his life and hold on to the good memories we shared. Best of all to know that he is now home, together with a cloud of witnesses and with Jesus, Hebrews 12:1. We are confident, I say, and willing rather to be absent from the body, and to be present with the Lord.

2 Corinthians 5:8. We grieve but with a hope to meet again someday.

Widow in the Church

The enemy didn't stop at my husband's death; he tried to destroy everything and everyone in the family. God's grace gave me strength to carry on serving as the Senior Pastor of our Believers Deliverance Church and also taking care of everything in the home. As prophesied by his father exactly two years before, before his illness Jesse joined the BDM team and preached his first message at our Christmas service. He loved the Lord and was learning to walk in his father's footsteps. He spent hours praying and studying the word. Our intercessory prayer meetings grew and God was doing amazing things in our midst. The first Sunday after his death, the Lord gave me a message entitled, "The Gift of Life." How could this be when I just lost my husband? But I obeyed the Lord and many were touched. We had the worst snowy winter that year, my little girl and I shoveled our four car driveway by ourselves. We were crying out and missing the 'man of our house.' I was clueless about so many things; even to fill gas, wash my car, (I drove through the car wash one day, what a mess!) and do handy jobs around the house. I was handling a lot; government, accounting and paper work for the Church, his death documents, grave site and as well as doing errands, trying to answer calls and finalize reports, etc. The next morning I went to the mechanics to get my van mirror fixed and waited in line for parking. As soon as someone pulled out of the parking lot the Holy Spirit said to me 'talk to him' and before I knew anything, I pulled down my window and said, "good morning sir, I want to tell you that Jesus loves you." I rolled up my window and cried out aloud, "O Lord why do You do this to me?" See, I was always ministering to people on the streets but this time it was different. I was sad, mad and did not want to talk to anyone. I spent hours in prayer. The Holy Spirit was my Father, Husband and closest Friend! The enemy was trying desperately to rip us all apart in our grief. On two occasions I had an out-of-body experience and the Lord promised me that He was in charge and I felt safe that everything was going to be fine. Both times it was very late at night and all I could do was pray in the spirit and weep before the Lord. Suddenly I felt the loneliness and my burdens were too heavy. In my experience, I came out of my body and soared high. As I was rising I saw my body getting smaller and smaller. It became very tiny and in my spirit I heard the Lord Say; "Those who stand with you I will bless and will soar like you and they who come against you will suffer the consequences. I am in control!" The second time I simply soared higher and higher and higher and didn't want to stop, but it was an awesome feeling. Not many want to hear of such supernatural things that only Christ can do. But I treasured them.

We had a family meeting with all the children and their spouses. Everyone was hurting in their own way even my three small grandchildren at that time. I tried to help and blessed the older children with large gifts and the younger two had funds for their further education. The oldest son was given his father's gold ring. I so badly wanted to encourage him to get involved in the family as his father always desired. This was not only an African tradition but also Biblical. At that time it looked good but not after all that occurred in the months and years that followed. He still harboured resentment and bitterness toward his parents no matter what I did. Our Church was growing; God was doing amazing things and although it was difficult emotionally for everyone, we still had the Christmas banquet that year. January 2008, we invited friends and Pastors from other Churches, for a memorial dinner to celebrate my husband's life. The children and the Church did an amazing job. They officially ordained me as BDM's Senior Pastor. But I faced a lot of challenges as a Woman and a widow in mourning. My husband Apollo already warned me about the destroying spirit of Jezebel when we had a similar situation while he was in hospital. Jesus also warned his disciples about of His death in Acts 20:29-30, I know that after I am gone, ferocious wolves will get in among you, not sparing the flock; even from among your own selves men will come... But little did I think it would come from within. I introduced my son to one Pastor who I thought would guide him in ministry and whole hell broke loose. The enemy raged wild through that opening trying to paralyze and drive me insane. The hardest thing is when you trust someone and they let you down. The man would come every day to pick my son from the home and not even talk to me. Many encouraged this eighteen year old to take over the Church. But God gave me the boldness to stand up in intercession and to trust Him. Even David who was ordained as a boy of maybe ten or fifteen took his position as king of Israel only when he was thirty years old. 2 Samuel 5:4. As a youth my son was not able to understand what his mother, a woman of my age with so many responsibilities was going through and no one was there to help him. He felt the need to comfort me and his sisters but he himself was a boy and was also grieving his father's death. My oldest daughter and husband suddenly abandoned their leadership roles and left the church. I shed tears in agony and could only cry out to God. I anointed the children's pictures and prayed protection, restoration and for our healing. I never stopped pursuing my children the best I knew how. I would drive around my daughter's school weeping and praying. I called every ministry and asked for prayer. But God was faithful in all His ways.

The Lord showed me that this was the same vicious spirit of Jezebel at work again that wanted to take my life like 'it' did my husband's. I was labeled all sorts of names because I stood up boldly and continued to serve the Lord. This has become a common attack on servants of God these days when someone feels threatened by your ministry and prayer life. This is how the enemy works, he hates leaders and prophets of God and doesn't like to be discerned or confronted. One sure way to discern this demonic spirits of control is to judge the fruit. Test the spirits! When they come and rebuke you for loving and serving your Jesus, the Anointed Christ because God Ordained you as an Intercessor, Prophet to declare His Truth and to be a Watchman/woman on the walls for the Kingdom of God, do NOT be afraid! Even if they call you 'Jezebel' get bold and weep, accuse them before the throne of God and watch serpents crawl out and burn in fire before your eyes! Jesus said, by their ☐fruit (actions) you will know them. Matthew 7:16, 20. Some ministers live double lives, in secret sins, divorced so many times, afraid of the Holy Spirit Fire in you, they deny the Holy Spirit of Power and Might in their Church and even in their own lives. Rejoice, the Lord is calling you to come out and go about your Father's business in the Spirit of Might and Power! One Pastor's wife came to my home Bible study group thinking I was Jezebel. Hilarious, I have never seen such foolishness. Because I looked different and talked with an international accent they disliked me. She left sheepishly when the group started questioning her and the fire of God brought her to tears. My Jesus is a great big God! No one plays with the Fire of the Holy Spirit! I've learned to laugh at instances like that one and rejoice even more. Through my journey the Fire of Christ's love has continued to keep me burning and loving people even more to expose the wickedness of the evil one and to release others to receive His Holy Spirit fire anointing that we so badly need today.

Finally I couldn't take it anymore and needed a sabbatical to rest. My little daughter and I planned to visit relatives in Australia and tour the Middle East. I called for a General Body Meeting with our Ministry Partners, the leadership, a few members of our Church and my children so we could discuss my sabbatical leave of absence, the leadership while I was away and to invite other Pastors to assist with the Church services. But the funny thing was the entire meeting turned against me. There were more than fifteen people in my living room that day, most of whom my husband and I had personally ministered to and blessed in one way or another. But not one could speak in my defense. I felt like the woman caught in adultery being stoned to death. I was already dazed and embarrassed, accused of what I did not do or for something we did as caring parents years ago to protect our rebellious teenage children from going astray. My oldest son was fuming and took his best shot to attack me with bitter hatred. I just sat there numb not knowing what to say, seldom allowed to speak. They supported my teenage son to run the Church along with his Deacon friend and everyone shook their hearts feeling sorry for me. But my Jesus, O what A Man of war, He gave me the strength to fight the good fight of faith on my face in tears and supplication for all the Saints. Not too long down the years just as the Lord had promised, each and every one of them in that room and some others suffered some loss or the other. I do not rejoice. But sadly, even Christians fail to discern who the real enemy is. As for me and my house we shall continue to forgive, love and serve the Lord. We know are not fighting flesh and blood but principalities and evil power in the spiritual realm but we have the power in Jesus'sa name to destroy them. Amen! The following year I was forced to close the church with a lot of difficulties, strenuous paper work and great losses. We had to give away every piece of equipment, the instruments and church supplies to other churches which we took years to build. I was left all alone to handle the final closing and distributions but the Holy Spirit of mercy and grace was with me.

God never stopped using us even in our pain and brokenness; me as a Woman, a Widow and an Intercessor and my daughter Rachel in leading worship and praise. We journeyed to Melbourne Australia, transitioned in Dubai and served the Lord together in Bahrain. In fourteen days, we ministered in twenty one different meetings, of various languages under the Full Gospel Church of Philadelphia. Besides that I ministered in counseling, healing and deliverance in our guest's home from early morning till the evening meetings, every day till the day we left. It was powerful and the Lord worked many signs, wonders, healing and set every captive free in Jesus name. Today the barren have conceived, the oppressed are set free and even Pastors and family relationships are healed. During this fasting month of Ramadan I was invited to Muslims' home and many got saved, one bold girl was water baptized and before she came out of the water the Holy Spirit baptized her. Youth meetings and the three day Women Ablaze Convention was powerful, everyone was touched and received restoration. Parents wept to see their children baptized in the fine anointing of the Holy Spirit. No one was able to stand in the anointing. The same thing happened in Melbourne as I continued to minister and break bread from house to house, in prayer meetings and preached the word, God showed up with signs and wonders of and Jesus was glorified. The testimonies are too many to share and they keep coming to confirm the prophetic word given by the Lord.

Exposing the spirit of Jezebel

Only one thing I can say about such immorality and filthiness pouring out of hell into the Body of Christ today, that the spirit of Jezebel is viciously working overtime, I was confronted by this perverted demon in a dream the day I was going to expose 'it' in my book. In my dream; "not sure who the man was but he was with me and walked through an open door into the next room and went into another man standing naked and bent over. I quickly closed the door out of fear and disgust then woke up and was led into spiritual warfare. This confirmed this brazen perverted demon is going to push its filthiness in our faces; we will hear more of it, see more absurd stuff on television, in the educational systems, in our governments and in public. In the last of the last days, the spirit of Jezebel will increase its filthy attractions of sexual perversion and immorality from the bowels of hell, through music, the entertainment world, media and the fashion world and push it in our face. ``And the serpent poured water like a river out of his mouth after the woman, so that he might cause her [the church] to be swept away with the flood." Revelations 12:15. Watch it, Satan is after your offspring and after your testimony. But God's people will stand up with boldness, expose and destroy this evil spirit like Jehu did in 2 Kings 9:30-37. As the Bride of Christ becomes whiter, an uprising of the counterfeit spirituality, the seducing spirit of Jezebel will manifest more actively to defile even the elect.

Jezebel was an actual person, the wife of King Ahab who was one of Israel's most powerful rulers. She caused over ten million Hebrews, to bow to Baal, except seven thousand faithful believers including Elijah who worship the God of the Bible. This one spirit was almost totally responsible for corrupting an entire nation and this principality is coming in full force against our nation and the Church today. I Kings 19:14-18. Although Jezebel is referred to as "she", this spirit has no gender and can operate in both men and women. It is an enemy of the body of Christ. It hates intercessors, spiritual authority and the prophets of God who speak the Word of God. It targets women who are embittered against men and can seduce and hypnotize a man just by one glance. It entices and leads millions of teenagers and young people astray through media, fashion, music and the lusts of the world. This arrogant, angry spirit is also behind abortion. But I have this against you, that you tolerate the woman Jezebel, who calls herself a prophetess, and she teaches and leads My bond-servants astray, so that they commit acts of immorality and eat things sacrificed to idols. Revelation 2:20. This is a controlling spirit and can direct lesser demons of homosexuality, lesbians and perversion to infest the Body of Christ. Like Elijah we cannot hide in a cave. With a double portion of Elijah's and Elisha's anointing and like Jehu we must wage war against the principality of Jezebel and destroy the demonic spirit like Jehu. While we must be compassionate toward those captured by her influence, we must show no mercy to the spirit itself. It must be cast down from its high place of influence. Indeed, as she lay bleeding and near death, Jehu "trampled her underfoot!" 2 Kings 9:30-33. Likewise, we must follow Christ and fearlessly walk upon this serpent, crushing it under our feet, Luke 10:19; Romans 16:20.

Some of you reading this have been made eunuchs, slaves to this evil spirit. Today, right now, God is giving you the privilege and the anointing to come against this controlling, immoral evil spirit. You must cast 'it' down and out! It's time for the prophets to unite against this spirit. Satan's ultimate hatred is against God Himself, he hates the grace God upon God's bond-servants, even after they sin. It hates the fact that God will use the weakest and lowliest and make them powerful in Christ's name.

Let us pray:

My Heavenly Abba Father, we submit to You and Your standard of righteousness. We ask for purity, meekness and holiness of heart. Forgive us for our sins, tolerating and allowing the spirit of Jezebel in both our minds and our deeds. Father, because we submit to You, we resist the devil and he has to flee. We bind the principality of Jezebel over our marriage, home, children, and the educational system; we pull down and destroy every form of wickedness in high places. We tear down the fortresses the Jezebel spirit has built up in the spirit realm and plunder the enemy's camp with the fire of God. We also break off the cycle of strife and rivalry in marriages, between siblings, parents and children, between Pastors and their spouses and in the Church. You evil spirit of Jezebel, in the authority of Jesus Christ we trample on you serpents and scorpions and render you powerless in Jesus name. We speak faithfulness of eyes and heart to husbands and wives. We release purity, the grace of Jesus and the fear of the Lord to consume us, in our homes and in our children, both single and married. We repent and ask You cleanse and sanctify us with the blood of Jesus. We destroy witchcraft charms, witchcraft sex, witchcraft division, and mind control over families and send arrows of God into hearts to destroy false love, lust, delusion, and confusion and replace it with the Agape love of the Father. We lose the joy of humility and a submissive spirit. We release every captive and set free the slaves in your hold by the blood of the Lamb of God, in Jesus' name. Amen!

Prayer and Intercession

Prayer is, having an intimate conversation of your deepest thoughts, desires and longings with God. No one else will understand, read your lips or can take this place like Jesus. He will answer every heart's cry, call and whisper. Prayer will cause you to have a great need to communicate with your Creator and to believe He is always there. After I made Jesus the Lord and Saviour of my life, I learned how to 'Pray Without Ceasing,' not in head-bowed, eyes-closed posture all day long, non-stop talking but rather an attitude of God-consciousness and surrender to Him Who alone is Sovereign. When your thoughts turn to worry, fear, discouragement, and anger, quickly turn them into prayer and every prayer into thanksgiving. Prayer should be like breathing. You do not have to think to breathe. Unfortunately, many believers hold their 'spiritual breath' for long, thinking brief moments with God is sufficient to survive. Intimacy with Jesus Christ depends on your communication with Him over every situation in your life. Pray when the time is now and you still have life and breath. Stop being anxious, instead by prayer present your requests to God, Philippians 4:6. Pray being watchful and thankful, Colossians 4:2. Prayer is our weapon in spiritual battle, Ephesians 6:18. Prayer should be our first response to every fearful situation, anxious thought and every undesired task God commands. Lack of prayer is lack of faith to believe and we don't spend time with God in intimacy. Unceasing prayer is continual dependence and communion with Abba Father.

Intercession is a Rare Calling

Groaning Intercession and tears are not of the flesh, yet done with our flesh man, the Holy Spirit is crying out through our spirit man. Some don't understand it or may think negative or even argue. But watch you do not mock or even try to explain the Holly Spirit's working other than the word of God. In the same way, the Holy Spirit helps us where we are weak. We do not know how to pray or what we should pray for, but the Holy Spirit prays to God for us with sounds that cannot be put into words. God knows the hearts of men. He knows what the Holy Spirit is thinking. The Holy Spirit prays for those who belong to Christ the way God wants Him to pray. Romans 8:26-27. The spirit of Jezebel hates Intercessors, Prophets and will viciously try to destroy, kill and stop this most urgent call in the Body today. The Church, our Families, especially marriages and children of all ages so badly need our prayers today. Jesus turned to them and said, do not weep for me. Weep for yourselves and your children. Luke 23:28. For fear many stop and hide like Elijah in the cave. I tried that too but it didn't work; the Holy Spirit found my weakness out and strengthened me. Now am compelled to be a walking cloud of tears to pray for others.

You can't stop the call of Intercession on a life. There is NO 'on and off' button or switch nor a set up time, stage or show. It is of the Holy Spirit Who cries out and groans through a willing, obedient vessel to pour out and preserve the earth your salty tears. You cannot put on, force yourself but only begin to Pray in tongues and invite the Holy Spirit to use you. Many can ask, bring petitions before the Lord but few allow, are ready, patient and humble to let Him groan through your spirit man. It does not look pretty, like contractions, hard labor pains and pushing labor in Praying. Most Warriors on the battle front, Prophets and Intercessor suffer rejection, abandonment and loneliness. Because most do not understand how an Intercessor is led by the Holy Spirit. Fasting prayer and weeping does make the body weak but the spirit strong. God jealously separates His servants to protect, preserve His anointing and to use His vessels as he pleases. Don't be discouraged! We die daily to serve a Loving, Most Powerful, Omnipotent Elohim, Abba Father, Yahweh God. Jesus showed us the way. It's not a choice but a calling. It's not when but anytime, anywhere all the time. Hotter the battle sweeter the victory! After Birth Pangs and Labor comes sweet uncontrollable, pure, complete Joy!

It is no surprise that though unplanned, this Seventh Chapter is the most important episode in the entire book and contains a lot of spiritual truths, secrets and revelation for the Body of Christ! Glory to God in the highest [heaven], and on earth peace among men with whom He is well pleased [men of good will, of His favour]. Luke 2:14, AMP. Seven is God's divine number! *Brothers (Sisters), I do not consider that I have made it my own. But one thing I do: forgetting what lies behind and straining forward to what lies ahead, I press on toward the goal for the prize of the upward call of God in Christ Jesus.* Philippians 3:13-14.

My tongue, He has made a 'Poet's Pen' in the hands of The Master! Let Your death speak more of Jesus than your life, a shadow that is soon passing away, in this journey of the living. No one boasts except in the Lord and King, from Whom comes every good and perfect thing. We are like grass glistening in the Son. Without, we are only dung, waste to be burned into ashes. But even from that dirt let your voice be heard loud and clear to glorify the Lord of lords and the King of kings; HE forever reigns!

After His Surgery

BDM's Multicultural Sunday

BDM's 7th Anniversary 2007

Silver Wedding Anniversary 2004

Niagara Falls

Chapter Eight

I walk out on my deck this beautiful morning and feel the cool gentle breeze clinging to my face. Trees, leaves dancing, birds chirping, grass glistening in its coat of green and everything feels so alive and well. The landscape is simple spectacular! Spring changing into summer is one of my favourite times of the year - dead grass begins to green again, sleeping bushes and my flower gardens come alive and look so beautiful. Wind, sun, rain and cooler breeze in the night. Living out in the country you begin to smell charcoal burning, barbeques, and signs of camping, kids playing, garage sales and heaps of outdoor activities. Then I wonder how such beauty from sleep and decay in the fall and winter months could grow right up again in spring. Seasons roll in and out, one after another, as the Bible says; to everything there is a season, a time for every purpose under heaven... Ecclesiastes 3:1.

We too live a life of changing seasons continuously sowing and reaping. I remember the seeds I had sown through the years; in tears, scorching heat, rolling in the dirt, bent down with the load and the struggles of life - they are beginning to show and make sense now. Lying in my hammock under the giant mulberry tree I watch birds of different colours and cute sizes singing around the feeders, animals grazing, turkeys are strutting about, wild rabbits running for their burrows and chickens clucking in the goat shed. It sounds like those fairy tales I used to read as a girl and thought they were only made up stories. But never did I think it would jump off the pages and be my story. Country living in a Western world, with God's creation right in my own backyard! Then I remember our prayers when we were in great need, 'O Lord everything belongs to you, even the cattle on a thousand hills is yours. Give us some of them.' For every beast of the forest is Mine, and the cattle on a thousand hills. I know all the birds of the mountains and the wild beasts of the field are Mine. Psalm 50:10-11. They have now become a part of my life and it's just fun watching each one with their own personality. Did you know that even little chickens are different each in their own sweet way? The old country music reminds me that I too can compose my own country songs. I can only imagine the host of heaven laughing with glee at this first time farmer girl scraping her knees; playing in the dirt, milking goats, doing my egg hunt and like little Miss Moffat in a nursery rhyme, I am churning my own butter and eating my curds and whey. Life has turned from doom and gloom to joy and bloom.

Overwhelmed, I stand in awe every day to see heaven unfold its richest blessings pouring into our lives. The Lord brought us to a land literally flowing with milk and honey and blessed us beyond man's thinking. Philippians 4:19. In His time, God answers every prayer and makes everything beautiful. Testimony after testimony confirm His glorious presence. My heart is bursting with thanksgiving to think how these temporal pleasures display heaven's glory in our midst. Indeed, "They who sow in tears shall reap in joy and singing. Psalms 126:5-6. Every tear God's stores up and will pour out to restore and preserve generations to come.

Family First Not the Church

Charity starts at home! Next to Jesus and loving God, it's the immediate family that comes next. A father always provides for his family. It's sad that Christian marriages and ministers of the Gospel are divorced some not once but one after another. A man's top priority is to be that God fearing loving husband first to his wife and a protective, caring father to his children. A woman is first a wife, then a mother before serving anyone else. Some have neglected their duties and switched roles for the benefit of fame, name, money and numbers. Husbands and wives work together in ministry complimenting and comforting each other not in separate ministries against each other. God made man and his own wife companions, helpmates, serving one another first then together reaching out to others. The opposite sex must be counseled and ministered to, together with the Pastor and his wife to safeguard your marriage.

There is a reason why Paul advised young Timothy to respect men and women. Little children are taught and encouraged to disrespect elders by addressing them by their names. Why a pattern of abuse, incest, course speech, addiction and immorality happens within a home causing so much hurt and pain passed over for generations. Do not rebuke an older man, but exhort him as a father, younger men as brothers, older women as mothers, younger women as sisters, with all purity. Honor widows who are really widows…But if anyone does not provide for his own, and especially for those of his household, he has denied the faith and is worse than an unbeliever. 1 Timothy 5:1-9. Maybe some are blessed to be raised in a happy and secure family with two loving parents. Some weren't, and growing up was tough without the love and support we longed for. Likely, as an adult you want a happy home for your family. Living peacefully in a family isn't always easy, but in God's restored Church, marriage and family is the most important fellowship you will need now and for eternity.

The scriptural order is God, spouse, children, parents, extended family, brothers and sisters in Christ, and then the rest of the world. When tragedy or illness strikes, it's the family who suffers most. It shouldn't require a disaster for us to know this truth. But too often, we let earning money, chasing pleasure, or even the needs of people outside our families divert our attention. Ephesians 5:25-31. If we are taught to respect each other regardless of ethnicity or skin colour, we have a safer environment for ourselves and for our children. We are all part of God's Family. Why we may call each other brother, sister, son, daughter and we mean it. We share a bond that transcends this life. God causes the lonely to dwell in families. Psalm 68: 6. Three things happen in a life: childhood with your birth family, your own family after you marry and have children and lastly when you enter into relationship with your spiritual family where you ultimately belong. In each family there is a head and Christ is the Head of the Spiritual family. Ephesians 5:23. Think about it, if you truly thought of your neighbor or coworker as your brother or sister, would you treat them any differently?

Meet the Man from Galilee

Today, many men and women are busy searching for what they call "success in life". They are down the valley and up the mountains looking for great riches, higher education, top careers and love relationships. Many in fact are able to find such if not all, but still are unsuccessful neither are they happy. Contentment is not in temporary things that are passing away. I've been there and done that too. Not until I met The Man

163

from Galilee, Jesus Christ; He gave me a new hope, changed my entire life and gave me peace. Before everything was He was. All that is visible and invisible was created by Him and through Him. Jesus was there from the very beginning. He is the source of everything. John 1:1-3. He had great love for mankind that He chose to come to planet earth in the form of a man. Jesus paid the price to reconcile mankind to our heavenly Father. Man violated His maker's law and accordingly was demoted and separated from God. But because of great love for His children, Jesus paid our debt of disobedience and came to save us from eternal destruction and from Satan's hell. The Love of Christ knows no limit, boundaries, conditions and no distance. His plan overrules every other plan of the enemy. God is jealously, possessively in love with us as His children because we belong to Jesus and we are His forever bride.

Trials and Persecution Will Come

True Christians cannot escape trials and persecution. Some will even face martyrdom for the Gospel. Jesus warned His disciples; ...beware of men...and the brother shall deliver up the brother to death, and the father the child; and the children shall rise up against their parents and cause them to be put to death. And you shall be hated by all men for My name's sake. Matthew 10:17, 21-22. We are the light of the word and the salt of the earth. A true believing Christian cannot be unnoticed neither can they hide their light. You will not even want to hide your light but shine it in the darkest night for all to see the way to Jesus. There is sweetness, comfort and prosperity in the gospel, but there are also fiery trials, afflictions, sufferings, persecutions and rejection. Apostle Paul knew this too well. Philippians 4:12. This was not because he lacked faith, but because he had faith to believe. True faith takes us out of the comfort zone into areas where we enter into conflict with Satan's kingdom and must demonstrate both patience and faith in the face of delays and difficulties.

All through my writings from beginning to the end, each day brought me loaded benefits from the Lord even more. But there were too many challenges and endless trials; many afflictions, sicknesses, fever, lung infection, fell and hurt my back, a frozen shoulder, constant headaches, threats, harassment, rejection, unexplainable heartaches and late nights because of the urgency in my spirit to deliver without further delay. God's abounding grace and amazing strength kept me relying on The Holy Spirit more and more every day. Nothing, no devil could stop this project. I started journaling years ago but early this year the Holy Spirit told me 'you will complete it' and He was going to work with me till the end and He did. The battle was hard one after another but God sent His angels of goodness and mercy to escort me, to hold my head and hands up. We will not escape persecution. Then you know the enemy has marked you and is afraid of your testimony. Dying a thousand deaths is never easy but living a dead life is even worse. Unless we overcome our own stinking thinking and put on the mind of Christ daily we cannot make it on our own. The Holy Spirit will take over if you ask Him. As I re-lived each episode, the wounds became fresh and started to bleed. All I could do is wait on the Lord for strength to carry on. In my human ability I had almost forgotten much of it, too much had happened in my life and the battles were endless. But as I worked on forgiveness and replaced it with prayer and love, the Lord refreshed me with the perfume of His presence. In the midst of it I was healed and refreshed again. Too many are the heartaches, attacks and afflictions of the righteous but the Spirit of the living God rescues and deliver us from each and every one of them... Psalm 34:19. The Holy Spirit brought every incident before me like I was watching a movie.

Too many difficulties came my way from all directions and as a lonely widow, I was falling apart. Hundreds of thousands of dollars was wickedly robbed off me by a relative when I visited Australia. I was in state of shock and grief from my husband's death when she invited my youngest daughter and me for a holiday. We went back a second time to live there for a longer period and then they worked the dirtiest trick on me. Suddenly I realized I was in a mess and lost everything just by one signature. But God supernaturally rescued me from this very evil situation and alerted me to quickly return to Canada. Miraculously in days I was approved for an apartment from January 2009, settled the children in school and rushed back to Australia to take care of this very stressful situation. I was like a madwoman pleading for my money but she refused and instead threatened me with a lawyer's notice to leave her garage, make-shift bedroom and stopped everyone talking to me. Strangers and friends helped me with legal advice and moral support. Many said I had a good case but my heart just couldn't take them to court. I took my case before the throne of God and He fought my battles, sadly they are still reaping the consequences till today. I took Communion and broke bread daily with the Holy Spirit, praying for strength and God sent me angels and strangers who literally come from nowhere and comforted me. I never saw them before and never saw them ever again. I started living out of my car until someone I

165

met invited me to their home. Another sixty thousand dollars was cheated off me by a so-called Missionary I sold the business to. He promised to pay me but disappeared. I became desperately depressed and helpless. I was not able to dress myself, comb my hair, think or eat. In the midst of my heartaches and losses, the Lord was blessing me tremendously. He started using me mightily all across Melbourne. The fire of God was being poured out on all flesh in homes and Churches where I was invited. We went from house to house breaking bread, having Bible studies, doing water baptism and the people were baptized with Christ's sweet love. One precious woman was an instrument in many of my meetings. Every day the Lord would direct her to take me to the most common places and people were waiting to be saved and healed. After hearing my life's story they would start shaking and weeping, feeling a burning fire over them and some would be healed instantly. Once a group of drunks we met got convicted, began to weep and ask God for forgiveness and received Jesus. Others received the prophetic word of knowledge (the Holy Spirit would give me details about their situation) and more people would come for prayer the next day.

Can one person endure so much? By Jesus' grace I did! I stand in awe of the mighty hand of the Holy Spirit Who never left me once. Death in my face, depression, loneliness, despair, cheated, suicidal, desperate, risked my own body, discrimination and racism, coloured babies almost given away, widow in the Church, sex exploitation, from rags to riches, ashes to beauty, grief to glee, sorrow to joy. On the altar of burning yet the Holy Spirit kept me blazing, standing, shining, with battle wounds, scars and all I can still smile and joy in my Lord. Forever to Worship the Great I AM and to show off His Kingdom glory on earth. God made me a voice to wake up the Church and the nations with the wildfire of Christ's amazing Love. The Holy Spirit is waiting, crying out, groaning for His bride. To draw His Children back to Abba Father's heart. Let us run together at the last Trumpet Call, abandoned to love, live to die for the Cross of Christ and pass on the baton of our faith to our sons and daughters, by birth and in the spirit. So Jesus is lifted up high, God be GOD and everything else like dung! O What great love to be called His sons and daughters, children of God. We are the Bride of Christ with oil filled burning lamps, waiting for our Bridegroom's soon return. Matthew 25:1-13. For now that was enough of weeping, it had worn me out day and night and now it is my turn and your turn to rejoice in our King!

After a lot of difficulty by mid 2009 I was able to reunite with my children in Canada. Supernaturally with the little money I had left, without a job and hardy any income as a widow, we were qualified to buy a condo. We moved into our own home by September that year. I traveled to Ghana on a missions trip and officially launched the Cheerful Hearts Foundation in Kasoa. I carried out missions and evangelism in Accra and in the town of Kasoa and had great meetings for days. We had crusades in the market and people were coming off the streets and being touched and saved. One drunken woman from the streets was directed to one of the meetings and God touched her. With power cuts and in the dark the African people beat their drums and worshiped God. We visited the town chief in his palace and he offered me land to build an orphanage and school for the country orphans. By the time I returned home I was exhausted and sick. I didn't realize then I already had symptoms of diabetes and my health has never been the same ever since. But God sustains me to serve Him anyway. My children were hurting, each one was grieving their father's death in their own way and we got little help from the Church. The first Christmas I was alone, helpless and not able to get out of bed. Yet the Lord would take me into His secret place of weeping intercession and speak to me in various ways. I read my Bible and listened to the Word throughout the night.

Angels are Real Helpers

Angels of Goodness and Mercy followed me 24/7. All my days in Melbourne I was surrounded with angels and a fire presence of heaven everywhere I went. I didn't need bodyguards. I felt safe that God was doing an awesome work in the midst of my tests. Years ago when my older brother was on his death bed in India and we were praying in Bahrain, that God would send ministering angels by his side and lead him to Jesus. He said two people showed up by his hospital bed, prayed for him and left. He soon recovered, got saved, attended a cousin's church and started serving the Lord for eight more years before he went home to be with Jesus. Once I was hurrying home on the highway in Toronto and a man honked, pointed to my wheels and motioned me to stop. He got out of his car, told me my tire was ripped and helped me fix them. He said 'take care' and drove off. I tried to race after him but he disappeared. Thank God he helped me in time or I would have had an accident. Angels showed up in various ways helping me escape from dangerous situations. Too many times our family was saved from violent gunmen and thieves.

I believe God's angels kept us safe, some men even among their group would speak in our favour and let us go. I believe angels do appear to people today. Be not forgetful to entertain strangers: for thereby some have entertained angels unawares. Hebrews 13:2. Sometime just as I am short of something like peanut butter or other food, people would show up at my door with exactly what I needed. Strange but true, my son once dreamed of boxes and boxes of cereal all over the house and funnily the Lord did exactly that. Every week our food bank in our basement would overflow with fresh bread, pies, baked goodies, etc., for our Church Community. Especially during Christmas and during the holidays, our van used to be loaded with all kinds of dry and fresh foods; fresh turkeys, potatoes and vegetables for every single mom, needy families and seniors in our community and in heavy snowy awful weather God kept us safe. Times our over loaded van would go wobbly and skid in the snow but somehow we made it home safe. Be encouraged that God's angels are at work. In special circumstances, we might even have one of those rare personal visitations. But better still we know that Jesus Himself has said, surely I am with you always, even to the end of the age. Matthew 28:20. Jesus, who made the angels and receives their worship, has promised us His own presence in our trials.

During this time I was hearing about Facebook and started using it as a ministry tool. Together with some of my friends we started a prayer group on Skype every week. I also had a Christian Radio Program and invited friends to join my Woman Ablaze group. Lives were touched and people were hungry, they called from all over the world. Some of those prayers resulted in miracles, healings, complicated court cases and divorces were resolved, Muslims and new converts were hearing the Gospel, others received jobs, finances, and deliverance and souls were getting saved, online! At the same time I would spend hours in prayer and speak the Word over my own situations. I would round my kitchen and living room praying in the spirit and calling back everything I had lost. The house was empty, my bills were piling up and loneliness started to torment me with suicidal thoughts. All I could do was simply weep before the Lord day and night and wish to die. I asked ministries and others to walk with me in prayer. I was having too many issues and was in much distress. Before I went on an outing trip with a group of ladies, I had written a suicide note and planned to take my own life the next day.

In one of my quiet times in prayer, the Lord promised me another husband who would run the rest of the race with me. I thought nothing of it but prayed and gave Him my list of what I wanted in a man. I was very specific this time with my list of spiritual and personal needs. One weekend my three grand-kids came to sleep over. While having breakfast that morning, my little six year old grandson suddenly blurted out saying, "Nana we need a new Papa, so you can be happy and my mum will be happy too." The kids and I laughed it off. But in the night before going to bed, Matthias came and laid his hands on me and prayed that God would give us a new Papa, we sang songs and I told them my famous bed-time stories. This was a confirmation from the mouth of a babe. I was not sure how that would happen. My late husband was a black African, the children and my grandkids are coloured and now? I had already many claiming to have heard from God that I was their wife but nothing had settled in my spirit as yet. One day, the Lord gave me the voice of a man who was going to be my husband. He impressed in my heart to write down my vision. Then the Lord answered me and said: "Write the vision and make it plain on tablets, that he may run who reads it. For the vision is yet for an appointed time; But at the end it will speak, and it will not lie. Though it tarries, wait for it; because it will surely come, it will not tarry. Habakkuk 2:2-3. I started praying for the new man. I broke off everything I didn't want in a husband and called in everything I wanted in a God-fearing man. During the drive to school with my daughter I would thank God for preparing a new father and a husband for our home. Today she thinks that was funny!

I got the same confirmation about my future mate from some of my prayer warriors. I received two prophetic words; one was from a sister in the Middle East I only knew on Skype. She pointed him out from my Radio program and another from an Apostle friend who prayed and prophesied over my life. He sent me a message one day saying, 'the Lord wants you to get ready for your new husband, clear everything out of the way. He is preparing the right man for you.' He continued on chat and said to me; "You are a mighty vessel of God. Fresh life is coming. New wine is on the horizon. The new wine will just be bubbling in your spirit. Let the oil of joy flow and every heavy spirit taken out of the way. You are into the fullness of time. When you wept, it touched the heart of God. Your tears are precious in His sight. Expectation of his coming is rising. You will still do foreign and local missions but you will have a solid base. Prophesy to the dry bones in the Churches he said - Ezekiel 37.

Again in a vision I saw two young elephants standing side by side. The male had his trunk out of a window in the stall. This too was confirmed by another Sister I met online. When I asked the Lord what it meant he showed me all the characteristics of an elephant; strong, gentle, slow but sure, powerful, his trumpet can be heard at a distance. He also eats grass; His strength is enormous that even lions and tigers are afraid and the elephant can crush anything that comes his way. When an elephant is in town everyone hears it, comes to see it and knows how powerfully strong the animal is, nothing moves him. Such was going to be the ministry call together with my new partner who was already at hand. Job 40:15-24. Wow Jesus!

Fred was reluctant to join the women's group but he did. He called from Michigan to pray for the USA and for his town every week. Earlier, we got to chat briefly and God was beginning to show me his heart and his hurts. Before reading his testimony, I had seen a little boy in my spirit with a lot of baggage from the past and God was healing him. We chatted a bit and he sent me his testimony. He was paralyzed from a nasty road accident and broke his spine and neck. He had to wear a halo with screws to his head for about six months. But God supernaturally healed him and he continued to sing in his Church choir with the halo until it was removed. So his life was a miracle too. The Holy Spirit connected us right away in the spirit. Fred called me on the phone and there after started our three hour conversations. This was the voice the Lord had given me months earlier. When I heard him I was afraid and excited at the same time. We prayed for each other and this went on for weeks. Fred was a single man and was prayerfully waiting for his promised wife for fifty years he said. His father was Italian and mother was a Native American, but he was born in the USA. He was a street evangelist also ministered in the homeless shelters and knew the word of God too well. I wondered about him. So I did a thorough check. We had a few mutual friends on Facebook, as well as his pastor and a colleague he worked with. They gave me a good report about him, confirmed that he was a 'born-again believer in Jesus Christ loving and serving the Lord and to my surprise told me exactly as I heard the Lord say about him in my spirit. That was amazing! There was no room for doubt, fear or even to wait as some would have us do. I relied on The Holy Spirit and trusted His choice even if my eyes didn't see it, but my spirit was at peace. A good friend drove me to Troy, Michigan. We met for the very first time and I though this man Frederick Spica was strange. When he first saw me driving in the parking lot, he dropped to his knees, raised his hands and started praising the Lord. I wanted to run back thinking he was crazy.

Jesus is Altogether Lovely!

Months later Fred came to Canada and we got married. Two Arab Pastors did our ceremony and blessed us in English and in Arabic. My new journey started on September 8, 2010. Only our Lord Jesus Christ could make such a match. All my children have begun to embrace Fred and we have had some great family reunions since then. We drove back and forth to Toronto for a few months and then I moved to the USA when I got my residence. It's been an interesting journey. As I write this report we would be soon celebrating our fifth wedding anniversary. God was amazing in all His ways and never short of surprises. Everything I had prayed for in my new husband, Fred had come out from and God was tremendously restoring us together. We are naturally different in many ways but have similar hobbies and find ourselves doing the same crazy things together. We like camping, fishing, watching the sunset on the beach and do lots of fun stuff together. He has blessed us with a beautiful home, a small retreat farm in the country and we have the joy to build it from scratch. One that jumps off my personal list is that Fred is a handy-man. Together we build decks, fencing, stalls and coops for our goats and chickens. We have learned to raise our little flock from birth, grow a vegetable garden and to live off the land. It takes hard work but it keeps us active and excited all the time. The Lord indeed is renewing our youth every day.

Marriage is not a bed of roses. Neither it's a snap shot but the most simplest things bring happiness between a husband and wife. Any relationship takes work, hard work, forgiveness and voluntary unconditional love. Marrying someone whose first spouse passed away is much different than marrying someone who has simply been divorced. Therefore, there are some extra things to take into consideration. We have had some ups and downs. As we grow older we teach ourselves how to live in God's kingdom by His rules so we can run this race together. We all have shortcomings but the Holy Spirit is a wonderful Teacher, Comfort and Friend and we trust Him. We married so we can be good friends and companions to one another as God ordained. A wife is bound to her husband as long as he lives. If her husband dies, she is free to marry anyone she wishes, but only if he loves the Lord. 1 Corinthians 7:39. This world can be pretty lonely alone.   As a young widow of fifty five I waited for almost three years for such happiness.   All my life had been struggles but now it's a time of rest, peace and joy in Christ's sweet love.   Indeed I feel truly blessed.   Not only was I blessed with a great marriage for twenty eight and a half years with my late husband, but now the Lord has blessed me a second time with another man after God's own heart, one who loves me beyond my wildest dreams.   My youth is being restored and I will fly on eagle's wings for His Name's sake.   God is altogether lovely!

From Woman Ablaze to Hearts Ablaze

After my marriage to Fred the ministry was renamed from Women Ablaze to Hearts Ablaze which continues the prophetic call I received in May of 2000.   Hearts Ablaze continues to move in the supernatural power of the Holy Spirit, manifesting in miracles, signs and wonders to restore the 'Body of Christ' back to the Father's heart.   We are all called to be 'Holy Spirit Fire Carriers', world changes, curse breakers, blood bought Ambassadors, called by God to impact lives.   On the last days, I will pour out My Spirit on ALL flesh, and your sons and your daughters shall prophesy.... Joel 2:28-29, Acts 2:17.   Among other things our hearts longing is to support Orphans, Widows, Young girls and Woman off the street and to build the Sum and Village ministry where ever the Lord leads us. Religion that is pure and undefiled before God, the Father, is this: to visit orphans and widows in their affliction. James 1:27.   There is a battle cry in our hearts through Intercession and Spiritual warfare to see many saved, healed and set free.   Fred I share the Full Gospel of Jesus Christ and many testify; they experience a burning fire, the love of God, healing of the heart, release from strongholds, peace and bubbling joy of the Lord. We too have learned through many tests and fiery trials to walk with God sun up to sun down.   We minister individually and together in homeless shelters, prayer meetings and online.   Jesus said; GO, preach, heal the sick, cleanse the lepers, raise the dead, cast out demons, freely you have received, freely give. Matthew 10:5-8.   The book of Acts continues even today!

The Word of God is true.   Wealth including money is a manifestation of heaven on earth.   For it is He who gives power to create wealth.   Deuteronomy 8:18.   Too long we were lied to and made to accept that poverty and lack is part of our faith.   Satan is a lying, defeated thief.   God has proved His Word is alive so we as His children are able to grasp our Father love. No matter how much man or the enemy has stolen from you, The Lord is able to restore and cause man to bless us a hundred fold over in each and every way. He is doing it in us and the same God will do it for you. Wait in a receiving attitude of the heart and watch your blessings roll in. Pressed down, shaken together running over. Luke 6:38. The more you give not only in money but also in prayer, your time, love and service to others the more you will receive. God wants your joy complete. God is a debtor to no man. Hebrews 6:10. There is no God like Jehovah Jireh; He cares about everything concerning you. Though your losses may be great His blessings are even greater. Rejoice and again I say rejoice!

Love Made You

Love is like pushing through until others see the baby's head and more, pushing until the child is born. Better still, even through the scars, bleeding and pain you can hold that baby and show off your miracle to the world. This is what intercessory prayer is all about. There is no giving up in your Christian walk. Giving natural birth is one of the most painful experiences a woman can endure yet there are many babies today who are living, walking miracles for Jesus. You are one of those babies delivered by your mother. Anything without pain is not worth fighting for. Easy come, easy go and you will not appreciate it and cherish it like you ought to. We cannot abort, miscarry or have still born babies who eventually die. Like Ruth a Moabitess widow who became the great grandmother of king David just by her humility and obedience. Ruth 4:13. As well as Esther a Jewish orphan, a courageous woman who risked her own life to serve God and to save her people. She became the Queen of Persia. Esther 4:14-15. You and I are born for such a time as this to birth forth great things in the spirit and to rescue the lost. God has unique strategies for you to fulfill the purpose that is on your life. He has ways that maybe you haven't seen done before or maybe other people haven't thought to do yet. Whatever God has called you to be, is extremely significant. L...ove, O...vercomes, V... irtually, E...verything.

I believe these breathtaking testimonies have touched your heart and will make a difference in your life. You will stand up and be a bold voice in prayer and in wisdom towards the things of God. As you seek the Holy Spirit more, the Father will draw you closer to Jesus and you will shine in His light. The fiery eyes of Jesus Christ will captivate your heart and prosper you in all things as your soul prospers. The Lord bless you and make you an extra-ordinary blessing to the nations!

I will bless the Lord at all times;
His praise shall continually be in my mouth.
My soul shall make its boast in the Lord;
the humble shall hear of it and be glad.
Oh, magnify the Lord with me,
and let us exalt His name together...

Oh, taste and see that the Lord is good;
blessed is the man who trusts in Him!
Oh, fear the Lord, you His saints!
There is no want to those who fear Him.
The young lions lack and suffer hunger;
But those who seek the Lord shall not lack any good thing....

The eyes of the Lord are on the righteous,
and His ears are open to their cry...
The righteous cry out, and the Lord hears,
and delivers them out of all their troubles.
The Lord is near to those who have a broken heart,
and saves such as have a contrite spirit.

Many are the afflictions of the righteous,
but the Lord delivers him out of them all.
He guards all his bones; not one of them is broken.
Evil shall slay the wicked,
and those who hate the righteous shall be condemned.
The Lord redeems the soul of His servants,
and none of those who trust in Him shall be condemned.

Psalm 34:1-22

Testimonies & Praise Reports

Encourage Yourself in the Lord! Never give up till the dead horse kicks! Have and ask God to increase your faith into stubborn, aggressive and receive the gift of Faith. No Woman has pursued her family, children, friends far and near like The Holy Spirit has strengthened me to do (times against my will) then and even more Now! No matter how hard, opposing, fiery the battles, hot, bodily afflictions are within and without, till your last breath do not stop praying, speak out in boldness and believe for the impossible. One day, you will see them standing at heaven's pearly gates as you cheer them in together with a Cloud of Witnesses. We may appear strange to the outside world, striving to be perfect, trying to do and say the right things keep in mind that only Jesus is The Perfect One. We shall be perfected just tike Him when we cross the other side, to live in His glory forever. In the flesh man, we often fall short because we live in a fallen world and in this decaying body. The hope we have is Jesus promised never to leave us nor forsake us.

No two people are the same, not even identical twins and no two people have the same miracle story. When you share your story you create a connection with others who cross your path or those who are facing challenges. People feel connected to your life and begin to think they too can overcome. Outsiders may look at people of faith and think we're cool with no issues of life. This is not true. Jesus Himself was tempted and suffered in every way possible till his death on the cross. The difference in our journey we learn to walk by faith and not by sight. We find our answers in the word of God to help us grow and have hope in a loving and merciful heavenly Father. We know if we confess our sins, He is faithful and just to forgive and wash us in the blood of Jesus Christ. The Holy

Spirit teaches us to communicate with God so we can pray in spirit and with our understanding. You create a trusting environment for others to share their story too. In the process touching someone who has not made a decision about Jesus. Your story can encourage others, exalt the name of the Lord and give hope. Even if your testimony is not that exciting to you, it can be to someone else. You have a story to tell. Whether it was a lifelong journey, or a moment in time that tested your faith, you can share that with many people. We are called to be overcomers, more than conquers and victorious. And they have overcome (conquered) him by means of the blood of the Lamb and by the utterance of their testimony, for they did not love and cling to life even when faced with death [holding their lives cheap till they had to die for their witnessing]. Revelation 12:11. Today, with the modern technology we are more blessed in many ways in which to do exactly this. You can stay at home and share from your computer like the ones I have received below. As much as the enemy uses the internet for bad, we can use this great tool for good and for God's glory. We have a voice no matter how young or old to bless, encourage and to free that one with what God is doing in our lives. Time is running out, days are crucial and dangerous for people in the world and the Holy Spirit is crying out to rescue His children as quickly as possible. Your shouts of praise bombard the enemy's camp and release a wildfire of Christ's love to the nations! Your testimony is what Christ has done for you. The Gospel is explaining what Christ has done for the person to whom you are witnessing.

Life Testimonies are Powerful

I am no saint, nor want to appear as one. Except that the Bible calls us Saints as Believers in Christ Jesus. As I shared the most sensitive issues of my life, I want you to know that a person does not suddenly change, overcome and overnight become a woman of faith. For me it was a gradual process. Yes I instantly and dramatically changed in my spirit as a Born-again-Believer when the Holy Spirit filled me that night in my home. My journey was one hard battle with trials and testing all the way. Till now, to shed off the stinking onion layers of my past has taken time, work and the fiery trials keep burning some of the unwanted 'fat.' I mean the old nature of the sin man passed down from my forefathers. It takes some of time to expose, empty and get rid of the garbage bag of dead bones but with determination and perseverance we gradually do overcome. God is still working in me. His love causes me to move on. We never reach until we have finished our race here and promoted to glory. I may have and give every reason and excuse for sin and the evil of my past BUT the beauty of it all is how God turned my entire destiny around. Through the years like a baby from milk to solid foods, we learn and teach ourselves from the word of God how to behave, walk, talk and follow hard after The Master Jesus Christ. He chose me fourth among my siblings from the womb to make a difference in this world. God handpicked me and plucked me like a brand out of the fire to use me for His Kingdom glory. He can do that with you too if you let Him. God chose Abraham, Isaac, Jacob apart from his twin brother Esau, Joseph from among his eleven brothers and David the youngest from seven who became the King of Israel in the Old Testament. But today, For whosoever shall call on the name of the Lord shall be saved. Acts 2:21, Romans 10:13. "And we are all the "Everyones and Whosoevers." There is nothing that can replace GOD's goodness and faithfulness.

Look What the Lord has done!

These praise reports display the lives of ordinary people who believe in an extra-ordinary God. Each and every testimony is published in good faith and with consent for the glory of heaven on earth. Many confirm the prophetic word given in ministry or simply testify of the goodness of God during our journey. Let the prophets speak two or three, and let the other judge. 1 Corinthians 14:29. One day you too will share and be a blessing to others. Only a Believer can boldly give a Christian testimony. One who received forgiveness of sins, salvation of the soul, healing and deliverance by the working and Person of our Lord Jesus Christ. God rewards honest labour, your labour of love to the Saints will be rewarded. The Testimony of Jesus is the Spirit of Prophecy. Revelation 19:10. Miracles happen in real life. Specific prophetic words were confirmed across the nations so you can get ready to receive yours now! And he gave some, apostles; and some, prophets; and some, evangelists; and some, pastors and teachers; For the perfecting of the saints, for the work of the ministry, for the edifying of the body of Christ: Till we all come in the unity of the faith, and of the knowledge of the Son of God, unto a perfect man, unto the measure of the stature of the fullness of Christ: Ephesians 4:11-13. Marriages on the brink of break up and divorce were restored. Barren women conceived. Deliverance and healing prayer online via Facebook,

Skype, Paltalk and other chat links as well as by phone and in personal ministry have confirmed the miracle power of a great God. Hearts have been mended off fear, abuse, emotional and physical trauma. Miracle babies were born, grown and some are young adults today. Most exciting of all are the reports from brethren of other faiths that amaze me, how the Lord saved, healed and supernaturally delivered them and their households. Glory to God! Praise reports keep coming in and some are from those serving on the mission field today.

- New Hindu Converts, a couple in Bahrain was waiting for a second baby for four years. During prayer in our house one evening, I received a prophetic vision of a baby boy. They got rid of their idols and received deliverance. Weeks later this Sister phoned me from the hospital screaming in excitement that she was pregnant again. We prayed on the phone and believed God together for the promised baby boy. Today their son Prem is doing his university in California.

- A Sister from the Church also conceived her second baby after receiving the prophetic word and was healed of fear. Her baby girl Sarah is now a teenager.

- A Brother working with my late husband Apollo came to the Lord after much prayer and fasting. Unmarried and in his mid forties, he was an alcoholic, chain smoker and had a vulgar cursing tongue. He came to our home for prayer one evening and the Lord showed me he would marry and have a son. He was drastically saved, got married to a young Christian girl and they had a baby girl. The second time his wife was pregnant it was their promised baby boy who is now about ten years old. Now he is a Pastor in the Middle East.

- A couple in Melbourne Australia were praying and waiting for many years to have a baby. I gave a prophetic word, broke the curse of bareness and blessed all the rooms in their home. By faith I told her to buy baby clothes and begin to thank God for their miracle. Months later she was pregnant but had a miscarriage. When I visited Melbourne a second time, I met the couple again in a Church where I was preaching. Prophetically the Spirit showed me that in 'three months' they will conceive again. Today the Daniel's family has two beautiful daughters.

- In Michigan, Fred and I were led to visit a family friend one Sunday. After lunch their daughter asked for prayed. The Lord gave me a specific word and the days in which she would conceive her first baby. Today praise the Lord she's a mother of two gorgeous children, a daughter and son.

Restoration of Marriages

• A Couple in Bahrain were having difficulty in their marriage bed. The husband was molested as a boy when a 'visiting preacher' stayed in their house and he walked in fear and torment all his life. God healed and delivered him from shame, guilt and fear. They now are happily married with children.

• A friend in Canada remarried and her new husband living in the USA refused to join the family. We counseled and prayed for the couple and now they are reunited, the man is blessed with a good job and they are a happy family.

• Hindu converts, a couple in Bahrain had serious sexual issues and perversion in their marriage. The Lord gave me a word for both of them. They and their teenage children received deliverance and the Lord restored the whole family.

Healing & Deliverance Ministry

• One young Nepalese labourer in Bahrain lost the use of his left hand in an accident at work. He had no feeling in his wrist and his fingers bend in, he could not open his hand. The palm turned black like rotten inside. Both hands especially his left is very much needed to manually harvest rice on the hills of Nepal. He did not know English. In one of our home meetings a group of us prayed that God would restore him. Apollo held his hand and I put a finger through his palm. As we continued to pray, gradually his fingers loosened, stretched out half way and the young man jumped up and started praising God in English. Two months after he won his compensation in court, God healed him completely. He learned to talk English and returned to bless us with his praise report.

• Once around 2am we heard a woman singing loudly on the street in Manama close to where we lived. Her husband quickly phoned us to say that his wife left the house half dressed and he was searching for her. My husband Apollo and I quickly ran to the street and tried to bring her to our home practically carrying her inside. This woman had too many demon spirits that entered her because her husband opened a door into their marriage. After weeks of deliverance with fasting prayer she was set free.

• Another sister in Bahrain met with an accident when on vacation in India and was literally demon possessed. She had every kind of spirit in her and manifested in wickedness. She was very huge and only the Holy Spirit could give us the strength to hold her down. After days of prayer and fasting she was set free. Her brother watching the power of the Holy Spirit in her deliverance got saved.

• A widow was delivered from grief and a monkey spirit that disfigured her whole face. She started manifesting in different voices but when the Holy Spirit touched her, she was filled with joy she was completely delivered.

• Months ago, a friend stopped by my house with a three year old Mongolian baby girl for prayer. Her ministry is to help bring physically handicapped children from poor countries to the USA to be surgically treated. This particular child only had some muscle on both her legs and arms. She moved only on her bottom unless someone carried her. We sat the child on the carpet and I began to prophetically pray for her miracle. Praying that God would supernaturally heal the child, grow muscle, strengthen her bones and she would not need surgery. Today, the little girl is beginning to walk with braces and to strengthen her muscle. We believe for her complete healing so her family and village can be saved!

• A very short divorced, Catholic woman was delivered from alcoholism, perversion and a religious spirit. She was tiny but became strong and violent, wriggling like a snake when we started deliverance. She came drunk yet the Lord delivered her that night and was beginning to do a mighty work in her life. But she refused to take instruction and out of guilt went into hiding and started living in adultery.

Keep Your Deliverance

Light and darkness cannot dwell together. Jesus is our Deliverer. The Blood of Jesus cleanses you from all sin and guilt. 1 John 11:7. Satan hates the deliverance ministry. Demons cannot touch the spirit of a man after one accepts Jesus, but they can work in the soul or mind of a person. Just like you can turn a light on in one room, and the next room in the house can be in darkness, the same is true in the spirit realm. We need to renounce and must cut off all legal grounds the enemy has before deliverance or it can be dangerous. The person can get violent and get hurt or hurt you. When the unclean spirit has gone out of a person, it roams through waterless places in search [of a place] of rest (release, refreshment, ease); and finding none it says, I will go back to my house from which I came. And when it arrives, it finds [the place] swept and put in order and furnished and decorated. And it goes and brings other spirits, seven [of them], more evil than itself, and they enter in, settle down, and dwell there; and the last state of that person is worse than the first. Luke 11:24-26. Jesus didn't allow demons to continue tormenting people who came to Him. Fear is a demonic entry not from God. 1 Timothy 2:7. Everything good comes from our good God and everything bad is from a bad devil. Most, ALL diseases, abuse, addictions, pain, lust, the occult, greed, curses, pride and fearing fear itself are tormenting spirits. Fear not, have faith in God!

Maintain your Deliverance:

- Lead a holy life - ...Be ye holy; for I am holy. Peter 1:15-16.
- Read Your Bible and mediate on the word of God - Joshua 1:8, Psalm 119:148
- Pray and talk to God - Matthew 6:8
- Resist the devil – James 4:7-8
- Testify about your deliverance
- Walk in the full armour of God – Ephesians 6:10-18

Breaking Soul Ties

The Bible doesn't use the word 'soul tie', but it speaks of souls being knit together, becoming one flesh, etc. It is a link in the spiritual realm between two people, which can bring positive like in a godly marriage – Matthew 19:5 and negative results when one is joined to a harlot or in fornication - 1 Corinthians 6:16-20. Demonic spirits use ungodly soul ties to transfer spirits from one person to another. Soul ties maybe be formed by sexual relationships - Ephesians 5:31, close relationships - 1 Samuel 18:1, vows, commitment and agreements - Ephesians 5:31. One young man had to break free from downright awful visitations from demons,

183

due to an ungodly soul tie he had with a witch. Another woman shared a promise bracelet with her best friend. When she became a Christian and realized that her friend's issues were affecting her she had to remove the bracelet, break the soul tie and was set free.

- Repent of sins committed with a soul tie, fornication and sexual sins are one of the most common ways to create nasty soul ties.
- Get rid of gifts given to you by others in connection with the sin or unholy relationship, such as rings, flowers, cards, etc.
- Repent, renounce and break any vows or commitments made in forming the soul tie even with the dead or living in Jesus' name.
- Forgive that person if you have anything against them and receive forgiveness.

Exaltation and Praise Reports

Praise, God from whom all blessings flow, James 1:17

Praise Him all creatures here below, Psalm 145:21

Praise Him above, ye heav'nly host, Revelation 5:11-14

Praise Father, Son, and Holy Ghost, Matthew 28:19

The Kataha family was a part of our lives in the Full Gospel Church of Philadelphia in Manama Bahrain. We enjoyed lots of good times of prayer and fellowship. My husband Brian and I were on a contract and worked as expatriates in the Kingdom of Bahrain for seven years. My memory of knowing Greta and Apollo was that they were Spirit filled prayer warriors and highly anointed by God Himself. We had weekly intercessory prayer meetings in their house and people got saved, delivered and healed. The Lord displayed His wonders, signs and visions upon us all during those meetings. One particular occasion they were planning to move and spread the Gospel abroad. During prayer, I being a visionary by the Lord was given a huge map of Australia and saw a letter on its way to confirm their travels. At this time, to no one's knowledge the family was already planning to immigrate to Canada. When we checked the Australian map upside down it looked exactly like Canada.

When Greta had her fourth baby girl Rachel Ruth in Bahrain, she never had to buy a thing for this child as God did provide everything. We celebrated Rachel's first birthday a day before they set off to Canada. Before they left Bahrain, the Church raised a love offering for their missionary work to support their travels. Am so glad we were able to reconnect via Facebook after so many years and are now grand-mothers. Am so blessed to be a part of Sister Greta's life and to see our children all grown up and blessed. I thank God for making me a witness of the mighty things He has carried this blessed family through. Every life will be touched and blessed by her miracle stories. Sincere Blessings always Greta, love ya!

Kaye Doyle, England UK

I really thank God for the burning fire of God over flowing in Sister Greta's life. I am blessed today because of Jesus and thank God for the teaching and training I received when I worked in the Kingdom of Bahrain. As an expatriate nurse I lived alone without my family in a nurse's hostel. After attending the Full Gospel Church of Philadelphia in Manama, I joined the English Cell group in the house of late Brother Apollo and Sister Greta. They also held prayer meetings, fellowship and other deliverance meetings. Sister would faithfully pick all the ladies from the nurse's hostel and drop us back with Brother late in the night. Our love feasts and fellowship in their home was wonderful.

After a very long time, I was able to re-contact with Sister again through my daughter on Facebook. We recollected on our fellowship in their home in Bahrain, the nurse's hostel bible studies and the prayer meetings. I remember her phone calls and encouragements to get ready for cell meetings. Maybe these are simple things for others but such reminders were marvelous especially for us new believers. We learned important tips of sacrifice and the Word of God. Besides having a family and children of their own, they made time to serve God and to visit people in need. I used to assist in gathering all the off-duty nurses together for the meetings in the hostel. Sometimes we went to the girl's rooms to pray for them. Many were getting blessed and began to grow in the Lord. Because of those days of training my foundation in the Lord became strong and now I am involved in the Ministry in New Life Fellowship, Mumbai India. God will reward you for the work of the Lord Sister Greta. God bless you!

Elizabeth Soans, Mumbai (Bombay) India

Recently I saw you in a dream Sister Greta ministering to people. This sister was a lonely widow with too many problems when we were introduced and prayed on the phone. We started a prayer ministry together online and by phone reaching many Muslims and friends. I myself am converted to Christianity and have a burden for people of other faiths. We visited homes, and prayed for many people in Canada. We witnessed many miracles and souls were getting saved and healed. God used Sister Greta's ministry greatly. She has desperate hunger for God and to serve His people worldwide. I am excited that her book of testimonies will bless people. I know you too will be blessed.

Hope Abukar, Toronto Canada

Back in 1999, I was at the movies with a friend and began to have a strange feeling in the pit of my stomach. I couldn't concentrate on the movie but suddenly realized my sin nature and thought, that if I was to die now I would be damned. That brought fear inside of me and I had no idea how to get rid of it. I was brought up in a Christian home with basic teaching and said the Lord's Prayer every night. But at that moment I was a sinner in the eyes of God. I was terrified when I got home; the only positive thing from that experience was me thinking, 'If I can get to Jesus I will be fine.' The problem was I didn't know how. I found a children's bible in my room but I couldn't make sense of it. The next day my best friend wanted to hang out. He reluctantly said that his mom, Sister Greta was having a bible study for the neighbourhood youth in their home. I jumped at the opportunity. He was unaware that God had been convicting me already. We went to the meeting that evening. I don't remember the message but my heart was receptive to whatever she had to say. She asked 'who wanted to be saved? Without a doubt my arm went straight up. I said the sinner's prayer and immediately the sick feeling vanished. I felt joy and that everything was going to be alright. My relationship with the Lord from the time was very dramatic. The intimacy that I experienced with Jesus in my alone time was very intense, I had just turned 19. God had completely transformed my heart. I was hungry for the things of God and started attending their Friday night prayer meetings and Wednesday night bible studies. I learned to pray, intercede and the doctrinal truths of the Bible gave me a strong foundation.

I became a member of the Believers Deliverance Ministries founded by late Pastor Apollo and Sister Greta from day one, since its humble beginnings in the basement of their home. I was baptized by the Holy Spirit and began to speak in tongues in that basement. As I grew in the Lord, I had the opportunity to serve on BDM's leadership team as a deacon, handling the books and witnessed many people healed and delivered first hand. Lucianne met Sister Greta through a friend and later got involved in her Women Ablaze Ministry and monthly breakfasts. She too advanced in the Lord and was healed in many ways. I was praying for a wife for the better part of a year with no results, trying to go about it in my own wisdom. When Lucy and I met in Sister Greta's house, she was the complete opposite to what I thought my ideal wife should be. Somehow by a miracle we got acquainted and a relationship sprung from it. Through the courting process and before our marriage, we were mentored and counseled by our Pastors.   Our wedding ceremony was officiated by Pastor Apollo on Lucy's birthday, November 3, 2007. Sadly, four weeks later he went home to be with the Lord. The ministry and mentoring that Lucy and I received are priceless and he is missed every day. Almost eight years now and we are blessed with two beautiful daughters. I will unequivocally concede that I am the man, father, brother, leader, husband and a believer today because of the BDM Church. Pastor Greta is a wonderful Sister in the Lord, a prayer warrior, loving and caring who demonstrates Jesus Christ, the hope of Glory. God bless her book that we pray will touch many lives for the glory of God.

Rudy & Luciane Adjetey, Burlington Ontario

Ever since God placed her next to me at a Benny Hinn miracle healing crusade in Toronto in 2005, Greta has been an inspiration to me. Our first meeting was very interesting. I shared how I had been feeling like I'm "on fire for Jesus" lately. These were very unusual words for me to use and I had never expressed myself in those terms before this day. She immediately became excited when I said those words. Her face lit up and said, "Guess what my ministry is called?" She then pulled out a contact card on which was written: "Women Ablaze Worldwide Ministries" Setting Nations & Saints on Fire with Yeshua's Love! I instantly knew that Greta was one of the answers to my prayer that day. Her heart was on fire for Jesus, her faith, and her experience with healing and deliverance ministry were a great source of help to me over the next few years as I was growing in these ministries as "a newbie".

In December 2007, I was invited to their Believer's Deliverance Church meeting in Mississauga. Her eighteen year old son was going to be preaching that day. I was blown away by the beautiful worship led by her two daughters, and how well Jesse preached the Bible. At the end of the sermon, he called people forward for prayer and many fell under the power of the Holy Spirit. I personally received a touch from God that night.

About a year later, I introduced Greta to three friends from my town in Angus. We all lived about an hour's drive north of Mississauga and went to visit her Church one Sunday morning. Two of my friends were a couple called by God to start a church in our town. It would be a Spirit-led Church that believed in healing and deliverance, just like Greta's church. After the meeting, all four of us went up for prayer to receive the fire anointing and take it to this new church being planted. We made a circle and as she blew on my face, I was instantly slain by the power of the Holy Spirit, as well as each of my friends. We knew that this was a sign that God was indeed, planting a church led by the Holy Spirit in Angus Ontario. Not only do we experience the presence of the Holy Spirit in the new church that was planted, but there has been healing, deliverance and angels singing among us there. Greta's friendship and generosity was also shown to this new congregation when she donated several items, including their golden communion set, to this new church.

I've had the pleasure of hosting my friend at meetings in my home a few times over the years. She has spoken several very specific prophetic words to me and to several friends, all of which came to pass very quickly afterwards. Just before my marriage was restored and my husband Harald returned to the Lord, Greta had a prophetic word from the Lord that we would be like newlyweds in a brand new marriage...and that is exactly what happened. I thank Jesus for putting this faithful woman of God in my life. She has endured much in her lifetime, but she has also been used mightily by our heavenly Father. Many blessings!

Doris Schuster, Angus, Ontario

We are first cousins from Kannur in South India. I've seen Greta grow up like a little sister. She was always active in drama, poetry and singing. I recollect her childhood of gracefulness even from a young girl. When Greta came to India a few years back she prophesied and prayed about a miscarriage I had. She was not aware of this except through the Holy Spirit. She broke the grief off my heart and I received healing. Her life has touched and encouraged so many people through the years. We are proud of her calling, the family and the ministry she does. Though she has suffered so much, Greta now stands strong for our Lord, building His kingdom on earth. Her many testimonies are true and life challenging. How God has kept her serving and praising Jesus is simply amazing.

Olga & Nelson DCouto, Bangalore India

I met Greta Kataha of Hearts Ablaze Worldwide Ministry on Facebook after I lost my husband. She shared in my sorrow and comforted me as she too was once a widow. Her love and attention helped me to grow stronger in the Lord. She would take time to share the Bible, answer my questions and pray for me online. We met a few years ago for the very first time when she traveled to Chennai on her mission trip to India. I had the pleasure to host Sister Greta in my house and accompany her to all her meetings in the city and in the slum Churches. Little kids came running to greet her. I organized a fellowship meeting in my apartment building and marriages were restored, people got saved and bodies were healed by the Holy Spirit. We attended a traditional India wedding together; a family Greta knew from the Middle East whose son was in Australia. Greta did the marriage counseling for the new couple in Chennai. We also visited many homes in the community and people's legs were lengthened, hands and bodies straightened and some delivered from evil spirits, including Hindus and Catholics.

I have witnessed Sister Greta move in great faith trusting God even for her finances. Money orders came to my house and so many gave her cash gifts to support her work in India. Am amazed how she totally depends on the Holy Spirit. She is lovely human being, a spirit filled servant of the Lord and a loving mother not just to her children but also to other kids. I wish her, the book and the readers God's blessings.

Arlene Ruth Peters, Chennai South India

A friend introduced me to Hearts Ablaze Worldwide Ministries on Skype when I was in great need. I am from a Hindu background and love Jesus very much. My parents are very strict Hindus and refused me to go to Church. They insisted that I worship their Hindu gods. A dove always sat on my window and I felt it was a way God was comforting me in my pain. A Christian colleague I knew used to phone me regularly to pray and teach me the Bible. When Pastor Greta and I first met online, I had a slip disc and was in great pain. She prayed and prophesied over my life that God will touch and heal me completely. The next day I was feeling a lot better and was able to sit up in bed. Only then did I tell her about my physical condition. Mom Greta prayed a deliverance prayer over my life. She said, get out of the bed, find another chair and stretch your legs. Right there the pain left my body and I was able to stand straight. Because of our culture and Hindu religious practices I was also very afraid of my parents. But after regular prayers with Mom, I got bold and was able to talk to them about my Christian boyfriend of last six years. With prayer my parents finally consented to our marriage and blessed us. I was completely healed and went back to continue my studies in medicine and got my degree as a doctor.

When Pastor Greta came to Bangalore on her last mission's trip to India, I was able to meet her face to face along with my husband for the very first time. God has led me to support Hearts Ablaze Ministries financially for her slum projects in India. Jesus did many healings and miracles in my life. Now my husband and I are praying and believing for a baby. I am now completely healed, active and work full time as a doctor. We thank God for the dedication and love of Pastor Great, a real spiritual mother to me. We believe and pray God will bless her labour of love. You will be blessed. Thank You Jesus!

Dr. Srija Sadasivan, Bangalore India

Aunt Greta, we are always blessed to read your posts and thoughts on Facebook. May our Lord continue to bless you and keep you in the best of health and provide all resources as you walk to build God's kingdom. Just to let you know people like us are really learning a lot from you. Thanks, you are a blessing to me. My best is to share this book with most of the people I know in India and Singapore. So your book with the truth of His word can reach the lost and win many souls. Love you, Take care and God bless.

Prela & David Susan DCouto, Bangalore India & Singapore

When the Holy Spirit tells a 91 year old woman to give Greta Kataha twenty dollars for her ministry outreach, then you must know how God thinks of His daughter. I have known Greta from the Women Ablaze conferences and breakfast meetings she used to organize in Mississauga Ontario. God is using her mightily for what He has prepared her for. It is a privilege to get to know and feel her heart for God's Kingdom business. Her life stories are amazing and uplifting. You will enjoy this book and be blessed. Thank you.

Helen Golbeck, Oakville, Ontario

Michael and I are family friends with Greta Kataha (Pinto) when we were school going teens in Erode, South India. Although each of us schooled in different towns, we met up for the holidays in the railway colony. Our fathers worked on the railways and we lived in an Anglo-India railway colony. I, Michael remember the Pinto family who lived across the street from our house. We were friends. As kids we played together, attended the Catholic Church in our town and went for all the dances in the Railway institute. Many times when Greta's father used to drink and turn violent, she with her mum and younger siblings would come to hide in our house. My mother Thelma D'Rosario can testify about the sad stuff the family endured until they were separated and relocated. Through the years we have all grown, got married and gone our separate ways. Years later she found us on facebook and never failed to keep in touch with us ever since.

Seeing Greta's life now, we are so happy and proud how God has blessed her marriage, children and ministry. She always has an encouraging word, exaltation, a praise and prayer for us. She makes us feel very special. We are still a family but now we have become even closer because of Jesus coming into our lives. Her posts on Facebook are very encouraging and up lifting. We love her, the ministry she is doing worldwide and her beautiful family. Financially we were blessed to support her when she travelled on missions to India. We are excited to see her book come real and to read her life stories. The world should know that our Sister is a true servant of God and the Lord has been faithful in her life. We are proud she's from our neighbourhood and we get to be a part of her life stories. You too will be blessed, encouraged and challenged to push through life and live for Jesus.

Congratulations on your Book, 'I Cheated Death!' You've made it through all your suffering and pain of growing up. God bless you more!

Michael & Jacqueline D'Rozario, Erode, South India

A vessel of honor, chosen and sanctified to be used for every noble purpose, is who I see Evangelist Greta Kataha to be. After hearing about her ministry, I met her when she came on a mission's trip to Ghana years ago. I assisted in the arrangements, organizing her Women Ablaze Crusade meetings and also in leading prayer sessions during the meetings. With the awesome presence of God, there was no way anyone could dispute the fact that this was a tested, tried and an approved vessel of God. Souls were saved, the sick and demon oppressed got healed, and lives were touched by the power of God. Even the less privileged in our society were blessed through her visit to some of our Orphanages and schools. Pastor Greta's love for God coupled with her great passion for the salvation of souls made her mission to Kasoa Ghana impacts our lives greatly. To me, it's a blessing to know someone like her.

Pastor Ebenezer Kwao, Ghana West Africa
Utmost Outreach Mission Ghana

My sweet wife Madhu and I have been praying and waiting on God for a baby. Aunty Greta is a cousin on my mom's side. One day she sent me a prophetic word on facebook in 2012 saying, "God is about to do something amazing in your lives, get ready. Get the name, stuff, believe and speak it. Begin to rejoice for it is here!" She didn't know about our hearts cry for a baby. We were overwhelmed with the news and thanked The Lord. A few days later Madhu went for a checkup and found she was pregnant. The doctors were uncertain because she had fibroids growing alongside the baby. This meant we would have to abort the baby or it could lead to complications. We were devastated with this news. But after a few more checkups the reports confirmed that we could go ahead and keep the baby. We held on to the prophetic promise we received from the Lord through A. Greta and did not worry about the fibroids. The Lord protected and kept our baby safe and little Jaden DCouto came into this world, perfectly healthy, born on 2nd April 2013. He is a testimony to prove, that what The Lord has promised no one can touch and the devil could not steal our joy. Madhu and I want to thank God for our family and our miracle baby boy who is now two years old and is a joy to us. We met A. Greta when she came to Bangalore on her mission's trip and took pictures. My wife and I believe and agree with her that this book of miracle stories will bless many couples as she has blessed us with her love and obedience to serve Jesus.

Madhu and Daniel DCouto, Bangalore India

We met Aunty Greta at a prayer meeting in 2008 when she was visiting Melbourne with her daughter Rachel and we were deeply impacted at that session. She had such a magnetic force that drew us to the Lord. She conducted many prayer meetings that we attended and we then slowly got to know her better. Her teaching and preaching always empowered us and stirred in us a thirst for a deeper knowledge of God. She was a very faithful woman of God and her life was a testimony of the calling that was placed on her. During her time in Melbourne we invited her to our house that was under construction and requested her to pray for our soon to be home. That day she prophesied that we will have a third child. We did not pay attention to it because at the time we had two boys aged nine and five years old and were not planning on trying for a girl or a third child. But two years later our third son Jadon Daniels was born. She even prophesied that this child will be a very joyful and will carry that joy everywhere which is true and we praise God for that.

Aunty Greta, as we fondly call her has never failed to praise the Lord and serve Him even in times of great trials as a widow. She always carried in her a fire for God. We were blessed to have her stay in our home for a couple of months prior to her returning to Canada. During her stay with us she shared so many supernatural miracle stories and times we would fellowship late into the night. She was always ready to teach us the Word of God and we were really blessed. She was a blessing to many individuals and couples and usher prophesies uplifted many people and gave them hope to look forward to the greater blessings that God had in store for them. We pray her book will be a blessing to every reader and can't wait to read the same.

Jimmy & Leena Daniels, Melbourne Australia

For sure my friend loves the Lord. An advertisement in the local news papers caught my attention to attend Greta's first 'Women Ablaze Conference' in Mississauga in May 2000. Late Nicole Brook was the guest speaker and we had a great time of fellowship, food and meeting new people from different ethnic backgrounds. Her youngest daughter Rachel did a beautiful interpretive dance. We are good friends and sisters in the Lord. For a few years, I was a member of their Believers Deliverance Church. We shared many precious times together; with her family, at the pancake feasts in my house and just praying. She never fails to keep in touch and occasionally visit me to cheer me up. May the Holy Spirit warm your heart as you read her miracle stories and strengthen you to receive your miracles.

Marion Ratz, Mississauga Ontario

We first met Greta in January 2011 when her new husband Fred (a longtime friend) brought her from Canada to stay at our home while they looked for housing near Grand Rapids. What we knew about her was not much. She was born in India. Her late husband was from Africa and died in Canada from an aneurysm. Fred met her online via her Woman Ablaze Radio program and prayer group on Skype. What we came to know about Greta was that she had lived a life that we could hardly imagine. A life with untold struggles, much persecution and survival that only occurred by the grace and mercy of God.

We have come to know that Greta loves The Lord with all her heart, mind and strength. It is her heart's desire to share the love of Jesus with as many souls as possible. She will use her own hands, feet and voice. She is ready to go to the missions field, (we were blessed to support her last trip to Honduras) and uses social media, radio and any other means The Lord will supply. She will even tell her life story if it will bring even one to the love of Christ.

Sue and Paul Schadel - Holland, Michigan USA

Dear Sister Greta, I am very excited for you and your book project. I can't wait to read it. You have a great way with words, and why not, the Holy Spirit shines from within you. Ever since Pastor Leslie Pinto introduced us in 2008, I have enjoyed our friendship, and as an author myself, I have followed your Holy Ghost inspired daily devotionals on Face Book. Again, I am excited about reading your upcoming book. Your storyline sounds great and it should make for an exciting and interesting read. God bless you in all that you do Greta, both with your family, ministry, and now your book writing venture. I see great things coming from this book. Your brother in the Lord,

James Lindquist (Warren), Albany, Oregon USA

Hello Madam, Pastor Greta K-Spica, I am the lady Pastor who waited on you when you visited Ghana, Kasoa in the Central Region some four years ago. You came to our church to greet us. I was with Mr. Eric of Cheerful Hearts Foundation in Kasoa, Ghana when your Woman Ablaze Ministry came for crusades and to dedicate the NGO. We have been thinking about you always I really appreciate how God involved me in your mission in Ghana; it has given me an answer to the question on my mind of how I can be involved in God's work by travelling. Now am ever ready for God anywhere and everywhere. Hearts Ablaze Worldwide Ministries, may God satisfy you this year with His Mercy and favour. May He give you fresh anointing to keep the fire ablaze continuously. We Love You!

Esther Oluwatoyin Nyako, Kasoa, Ghana West Africa

Since 1996, we have known Greta and her family. We met in Mississauga Gospel Temple and had good fellowship ever since. Our two sons are friends from a very young age. We were led to bless the family with food, warm clothing and to support their ministry. Later in the years we became members of their Believers Deliverance Church till they closed the church. This multicultural gathering of people from different faiths and ethnic groups was a blessing to us as we labored together in the Lord. For years we have witnessed God using this family, among new immigrants, women and families in healing and deliverance in our community.

We have had the pleasure to pray and walk with Greta through the family's greatest loss; of our Pastor and dear friend and also during the years when she was a widow. We attended her son Jesse's wedding and celebrated her marriage to Fred Spica as well. We thank God for her life and the supernatural miracles the Lord continues to do in Hearts Ablaze Worldwide Ministries. We know you too will be blessed by her testimonies. We bless you and pray God uses you more for His glory. Congratulations!

Dale & Roeli Lutz, Mississauga Ontario.

I know Greta Kataha from our Catch the Fire Church in the Mississauga. She was a part of our weekly cell group. As we grew closer in fellowship and prayer, I witnessed the amazing things the Lord has being doing in her life. As a widow, she was very lonely and depressed. She has suffered too many losses and much rejection that she became suicidal. One day she suddenly came to my house weeping and asking for prayer wanting to die. But I have seen how the Lord has carried her through. We had a lot of celebrations together, including her wedding to Fred which was an amazing miracle. Recently on Victoria Day, Greta was led to pass by my house on her drive from Canada. To her surprise we were having a birthday party for the daughter of a Ugandan family she too knew well. Everyone was happy to see her. We had a great time of food and fellowship.

We enjoy each other's company and are good prayer partners. It is a constant amazement to me how she carries the fire of God wherever she goes. I thank God for her life stories and I am blessed with her God experiences.

Elli Murack, Mississauga, Ontario

My husband Suheil and I know Greta Kataha through an Arab friend from Somalia, now in Canada. We used to meet for prayer. Many Brothers and Sisters blessed us with prayer and encouragement. For seven years we believed God for a baby. Pastor Greta Kataha prophesied over our marriage and prayed for my womb. She said God was going to bless us and I will conceive in the coming months. One year and a half later I conceived and today we are blessed with a twin son and daughter of four and a half years.

Again Greta and our friend came to our home and we prayed in the basement. My mother was down by the Holy Spirit, started laughing with joy and praying in tongues. At this time my mom was suffering with Lymphoma cancer. Before we left to Syria, my mother saw the Lord hands in a dream and her healing was made complete. Greta anointed our house and prayed for my whole family. We were blessed to support her Hearts Ablaze mission work in Honduras. Thank God for her life. We give God all glory for touching us and anointing His servants to do His work. We know many others will be blessed with Greta's book of testimonies.

Fadia & Suheil Dirani, Brampton Ontario

Aunty Greta my mama is a simple lady and you are the bolder person. I learn in the flesh to be like her and with the power of the Holy Spirit to be bold like you. I love to read and learn from your Facebook posts. My Mama always carried the hurt of a miscarriage and praise God she is set free and healed by the Holy Spirit who revealed it through you. I like to share an extract from a poem the Lord inspired me to write from my own life experience to comfort married women who may encounter unexpected pregnancies and feel lonely in this world. Be encouraged and inspired for a child is not planned by human mind and efforts but by our Heavenly Father. Jeremiah 29:11 For I know the thoughts that I think toward you, saith the Lord, thoughts of peace, and not of evil, to give you an expected end.

My Joy Unknown

(Composed by Diana (Dcouto) Samuel)

My little son is such a joy, he makes us always smile
He has a way to touch our hearts, the Lord made him the best
When I look back at time, when he was planted in my womb
I was never overjoyed, but felt a burden deep within
I measured everything, with worldly knowledge as the scale
Everything was so incorrect I admit I messed up.

Today my little boy has grown, to warm my heart which was torn
Had I remained rooted in my ways, I would not be joyful today
Coz God has made plans so great, for me to enjoy each new day
I cherish my boy so much today; he's my gift so dear.

Diana Samuel (Dcouto), Bangalore & Dubai UAE

Am excited to hear of your book, which will be a 'best seller!' I stand in agreement with you on that. Am honoured to be your friend and sister in the Lord. So blessed with your Honduras report, I got to be a part of as the Lord led me to support your Hearts Ablaze Worldwide Missions. Your Face book posts are part of my daily devotion, Anointed!!! There's just something about the way you write these things that causes my spirit man to soar! If I could I would stay on your posts and other encouraging ones and study His word all day. Am so hungry, I want to eat the pages sometimes! Ha ha ha ha! You are loved. You inspire me. I want to shout and praise God in HIS presence with you. Can't sit back any more and watch this worldly kingdom prosper. Yes, the Body of Christ needs to wake up and take what is rightfully ours. I am SO thanking God for people like you, Sister Greta, who I can connect with and be taught what I have longed to know for way too long.

Sandra Sanders, Michigan USA

Uncle Apollo Kataha is my late father Grace Kahoza's youngest brother. They were very close like twins, I heard growing up. I lost my father one week before I was born and Uncle Apollo tried hard to help the family; his mother till she died and his widow sisters. We are blessed to know his wife, Pastor Greta Kataha who I personally met when she came to Uganda for my Grandmother's funeral in 2005. I had the pleasure to meet her again when she visited Dubai. We spent lots of good times together, she treated me like a son and left me with a contact of her sister's family where am also a son. I am so proud with my Uncle Apollo's family and Children, who are my first cousins. We love as brothers. I am proud my mummy Greta is writing a Book that will help our whole family to draw closer together and have a beautiful family record for generations. As children we heard from my late mother and aunties (my mother died when I was five years old) how this mum had suffered many things in Uganda. But the fact is all what happened to her, she never left my uncle and the family, only to hold his hand and show him a promising life till his death. We love her and her new husband Fred Spica, especially my Cousins - Belinda, Roy, Jesse and Rachel. I am excited to be a part of their lives. God will bless us again as a family after all we suffered, lost and have overcome. Thank You Jesus! We always thank Him for raising us from dust to gold.

Beinomugisha Regan, Kampala Uganda & Dubai UAE

Testimonies confirm the prophetic word received and given out by His servants. But none of these things move me; neither do I esteem my life dear to myself, if only I may finish my course with joy and the ministry which I have obtained from [which was entrusted to me by] the Lord Jesus, faithfully to attest to the good news (Gospel) of God's grace (His unmerited favor, spiritual blessing, and mercy). Acts 20:24. Thanks for sharing your testimonies and praise reports with us. For letting glimpses of your life story touch others. One who knows and sees the bigger picture is the Holy Spirit and what is done in secret, He will reward you openly. You have lifted another soul from bondage, blessed others to believe and held a brother, a sister's hand and helped them to overcome. We all need somebody. You and I are given the boldness to be God's somebody for someone else. Be proud of yourself and rejoice! On that day, many will come to greet you at heaven's pearly gates and say, thank You!

Hearts Ablaze
Worldwide Ministries

Hearts Ablaze Worldwide Ministries is dedicated to go into all the world and fulfill the Great Commission of our Lord Jesus Christ. We are dedicated to preach and teach the Good News of the saving grace of God with miracles, signs and wonders with the entire package of Salvation to the lost. And He said to them, *"Go into all the world and preach and publish openly the good news (the Gospel) to every creature [of the whole human race]. He who believes [who adheres to and trusts in and relies on the Gospel and Him Whom it sets forth] and is baptized will be saved [from the penalty of eternal death]; but he who does not believe [who does not adhere to and trust in and rely on the Gospel and Him Whom it sets forth] will be condemned. And these attesting signs will accompany those who believe: in My name they will drive out demons; they will speak in new languages; They will pick up serpents; and [even] if they drink anything deadly, it will not hurt them; they will lay their hands on the sick, and they will get well."* Mark 16:15-18 AMP.

Please contact us at: heartsablaze@rocketmail.com for ministry updates, to schedule conferences, conventions, breakfast meetings, marriage, family, youth and deliverance sessions so together we can encourage, empower and equip the Body of Christ with the resurrection power of the Holy Spirit.

You may also partner with us for our various outreach programs to; Orphans, Widows, helping Girls off the streets as well as our Village and Slum Projects. We are running out of time, the fields are ripe and ready for harvest. Let's Go, Run, Deliver, Set Free and Rejoice in the Fire of Christ's amazing love! Thank Your for your prayers, sacrifice of love and support in our Kingdom journey together! Blessings of joy!

There's room at the cross for you
There's room at the cross for you
Though millions have come, there's still room for one
Yes there's room at the cross for you.

The hand of my Saviour is strong
And the love of my Saviour is long
Through sunshine or rain, through loss or in gain,
The blood flows from Calvary to cleanse every stain.

Chorus

There's room at the cross for you
There's room at the cross for me
Though millions have come, there's still room for one
Yes there's room at the cross for us
Yes there's room at the cross for you.

Made in the USA
San Bernardino, CA
21 September 2015